THE ILLUSTRATED REFERENCE

ON

CACTI AND OTHER SUCCULENTS

VOLUME FIVE

By Edgar Lamb

THE ILLUSTRATED REFERENCE ON CACTI AND OTHER SUCCULENTS
—Vol. I (1955)
—Vol. II (1959, 1973)
—Vol. III (1963, 1971) (with Brian Lamb)
—Vol. IV (1966, 1975) (with Brian Lamb)

By Edgar and Brian Lamb

POCKET ENCYCLOPAEDIA OF CACTI IN COLOUR
INCLUDING OTHER SUCCULENTS (1969)

COLOURFUL CACTI AND OTHER SUCCULENTS OF THE DESERTS (1974)

POPULAR EXOTIC CACTI IN COLOUR (1975)

also

Photographic Reference Plates on Cacti and other Succulents

THE ILLUSTRATED REFERENCE ON

CACTI & OTHER SUCCULENTS

VOLUME FIVE

written and photographed by

EDGAR and BRIAN LAMB

BLANDFORD PRESS

POOLE   DORSET

Copyright 1978 © Blandford Press Ltd,
Link House, West Street,
Poole, Dorset BH15 1LL

ISBN 0 7137 0852 2

ACKNOWLEDGEMENTS

In addition to further help from those mentioned on the similar pages in Volumes I, II, III and IV, we should also like to express our very grateful thanks to:

> Mr and Mrs A. Blackburn (U.S.A.)
> Mr and Mrs P. Forrester (U.S.A.)
> Mr and Mrs E. Gay (U.S.A.
> Mr and Mrs D. Johnson (U.S.A.)
> Mrs S. Holmes (née Carter) (U.K.)
> Mr. J. Lavranos (S. Africa)

for much useful data and help in many other ways. All this has added to the information which we have compiled over the years since the publication of Volumes I, II, III and IV, and which is now incorporated here.

E. L. AND B. L.

Special thanks also to Mr Les Fuller of 9, Thackeray Road, Worthing, who developed and printed all the black and white photographs for us.

Set and printed in Great Britain by Butler & Tanner Ltd, Frome and London

CONTENTS

COLOUR PLATES

*Owing to make-up it has not been possible
in every case to place the colour plates
entirely in Group sequence*

BLACK AND WHITE PLATES

Plate Nos. and Page Nos. continue from Volume Four

PART ONE: CACTI

PART TWO: SUCCULENTS

PREFACE

Since the publication of Volume IV in 1966, many changes have taken place in the cactus hobby, not least the introduction of many previously rare species into general cultivation. This has come about in two ways, one being through increased exploration work in the remoter areas of Africa, as well as in Central and South America. As a result, seeds have been brought back in sufficient quantities for propagation work, thus helping conservation. The other way has been aided by better and more modern methods of propagation, which in turn has only been possible through the tremendous increase in the number of serious enthusiasts in this hobby.

In addition to these previously rare species, many wonderful new plants have been discovered and named, including a number of very floriferous miniature-growing cacti, which are already quite common in collections in many parts of the world. Examples of these are *Mammillarias goldii*, *saboae* and *theresae*, which come from Mexico. In fact, in this volume, the Mammillaria Group is quite a major section of the book.

In the last twelve years, we ourselves have been on a number of extensive expeditions to Florida, the West Indies, and the desert regions of the U.S.A. and Mexico. For the first time we are incorporating in this reference series a number of colour illustrations, photographed in habitat, depicting mature specimens so that they can be compared in certain instances with more juvenile ones shown in black and white. These expeditions have also enabled us to aid conservation with the collection of seed of certain rare species, which we in turn have grown and distributed—not only to amateur enthusiasts, but also to botanical gardens and other like-minded institutions in all parts of the world. Certain examples of these are included in this volume, including *Echinocereus melanocentrus* from a very small location in Texas; also *Pilosocereus keyensis*, *Harrisias fragrans* and *simpsonii* from Florida. These latter three species are seriously threatened, purely through present-day land requirements for building development.

Although members of the Melocactus Group require rather higher winter minimum temperatures, quite a range of these species have become available in seed form in recent years. Many species in the genus *Melocactus* are now commonplace in collections, along with *Discocacti* and *Buiningias*, mostly as relatively young plants without their unusual cephaliums. We have been growing and studying these more sensitive plants for very many years, such that 17 species in this group have been included.

In preparing this long-awaited volume and because so many fine new plants are in cultivation, it has presented us with quite a problem as to what genera and species should or should not be included. We have, in fact, included a further 39 genera amongst the 185 half-tone and the 100 colour plates, which have not been illustrated in the previous four volumes. These illustrations have all been taken within 'The Exotic Collection', with the exception of the habitat illustrations, which have been filmed by us on various occasions,, some even during our last safari to Mexico in 1976.

Because of the ever increasing production costs, the actual lay-out of this volume is somewhat different to the previous four, whereby the colour illustrations are not distributed throughout the book. However, by including them as a section in the middle of the book, it has been possible to include an identical amount of colour to the previous volume. We feel sure that readers will appreciate the reasons for this change, even though more cross-references are needed.

Also, due to the increased costs of heating there has been a steady increase in the interest taken in 'hardy cacti', that is species which can be grown not only in an unheated greenhouse, but also in the open air, where temperatures can fall below $0°F$ ($-18°C$). Two half-tone illustrations accompany a chapter on this subject, along with a list of species on page 1369.

Worthing, England   EDGAR AND BRIAN LAMB

OPUNTIA GROUP

Some 55 species within this group have been included in the previous four volumes, hence the rather reduced number of additions in this volume.

In addition to including another species of *Pterocactus* and some additional species of *Opuntia*, the genus *Pereskiopsis* is introduced here with two species—*P. porteri* from Sinaloa and Baja California and also *P. velutina* from the Queretaro area of Central Mexico. These are interesting plants to grow, even if you do not allow them to grow to their full size, as cuttings can always be taken and rooted (for use as stock for grafting small cacti plants and seedlings). The flat graft system is usually adopted when using a stock of this type, but it is far better than *Pereskia*.

In Volume II, *Pterocactus kuntzei* K. Sch. was included and we would like now to refer this as *Pterocactus tuberosus* B. & R., the name by which it is known today.

In these days of high fuel costs, many people tend to forget about the genus *Opuntia*, because of lack of space in a small heated greenhouse. However, more and more people are realising that there are quite a variety of species of *Opuntia* which can be grown in the open air in cold climates where temperatures fall even below 0°F (−18°C). We are including in this volume *Opuntia rhodantha*, a very variable species not only in plant form, but also in respect of its flower colour and is shown in Plate CCXCVI.

Pereskiopsis porteri *B. & R.*
(Baja California and N.W. Mexico)

COLOUR: Older stems brown and woody, new ones dark green with bright green leaves

SIZE: Shown at about one-quarter natural size.

FLOWER: About 1½ in (3.75 cm) in diameter, yellow, petals rather broad.

NOTE: Strong, free branching shrub up to 4 ft (1.3 m) in height, developing quite stout stems with prominent brown areoles full of glochids and on the older stems 1 or 2 spines up to 2 in (5 cm) in length. These spines are green in the first year, changing to dark brown. The succulent leaves appear on the current year's growth, dropping off for the dormant winter period.

It is an exceedingly easy growing species, growing in any reasonable soil, needs plenty of water during the warmer months of the year, none in winter when a minimum of 45°F (8°C) is usually sufficient.

Pereskiopsis velutina   *Rose.*
(Mexico)

COLOUR: Green stems becoming brown with age as they become barky and bright green fleshy leaves, with a few white hairs and glochids.

SIZE: Shown at about natural size.

FLOWER: About 1 in (2.5 cm) long, bright yellow.

NOTE: As with *P. porteri* it grows as a freely branching shrub up to 4 ft (1.3 m) in height, but is considerably weaker in habit, forming into compact bushes. The aeroles bear several short spines and glochids as well as quite prominent long white hairs. The leaves are very succulent unlike those of most Pereskias, but drop for the cooler dry winter months.

It is a very easy species to grow, coping with any reasonable type of soil and enjoying plenty of water from spring to autumn. In winter a minimum temperature of 45°F (8°C) is usually sufficient when they can be left dry. In warmer climates, in the winter months, provided it has water, it will continue growing throughout the year.

Pterocactus fischeri *B. & R.*
(Patagonia and Argentina)

COLOUR: Grey-brown body with white areoles and radial spines, plus a few yellowish-brown papery centrals.

SIZE: Shown at just over half natural size.

FLOWER: 1½ in (3.75 cm) across, yellow produced singly at the tip of a stem.

NOTE: A far from common species in cultivation, despite the fact that it was originally described in 1920. It is a tuberous rooted species as with the other members of the genus. However, it produces short erect cylindrical stems. The production of the 3 or 4 papery central spines is very intermittent. It is also a shy flowerer in European cultivation.

It is, however, quite easy to grow, although slow, requiring a slightly sandy humus growing mixture, average watering during spring to autumn, less if the weather is dull and cool.

In winter, if it is kept dry, it is quite safe down to near freezing, even in a damp climate such as that of the British Isles. In its native habitat, where the climate is relatively dry in winter, it endures temperatures below freezing point.

Opuntia microdasys fa. cristata *Hort.*
(Mexico)

COLOUR: Light green pads with golden-yellow glochids.

SIZE: Shown at about one-third natural size.

FLOWER: Pale yellow and about 1½ in (4 cm) in diameter.

NOTE: The normal plant is very similar in appearance to the illustration of *O. microdasys fa. alba* shown on page 40 in Volume I. The cristate form as seen by the illustration above produces these wavy contorted pads instead, and a plant will eventually grow into a huge mound as you can see by the colour illustration in Plate CCXCV, shown at one-twelfth natural size.

It is of easy culture as are most Opuntias, whether they are normal or cristate, and will grow in any reasonable soil. It enjoys plenty of water from spring to autumn, but should be left dry for the winter months, when a minimum of 40°F (5°C) is sufficient.

Opuntia molesta   *Brandeg.*
(Baja California and Mexico)

COLOUR: Fresh green joints with a little yellowish wool and similar coloured glochids at the areoles, along with light golden-brown sheathed spines.

SIZE: Shown at about two-thirds natural size.

FLOWER: About 2 in (5 cm) in diameter, purplish-red.

NOTE: It is of easy culture and will grow virtually in any reasonable soil; it enjoys plenty of water during the warmer months, when growth can be quite quick. It will eventually grow into a bush up to 6 ft (2 m) in height.

In winter, it is best kept dry, when it is safe down to 40°F (5°C). The joints are very easily detached at this time of year as with the other related species, so plants should not be moved around unduly when pot-grown.

This species belongs to the Cylindropuntia Section of the genus.

Opuntia rhodantha *Sch.*
(Central and Western U.S.A.)

COLOUR: Green pads sometimes tinged with purple when in sun, with brown spines and glochids.

SIZE: Shown at about one-third natural size.

FLOWER: See Plate CCXCVI (one-twelfth natural size).

NOTE: This is quite a widespread species, often found at around 6,000–7,000 ft (3,000–3,300m), where they endure severe frosts as well as snow during the winter months, making this an ideal species for outside culture.

The pads vary from 4 to 6 in (10 to 15 cm) in length, and not much less in width. There can be up to 6 or 7 strong spines, the longest sometimes exceeding 2 in (5 cm) in length. Provided a very well drained soil is used, this plant can be grown in the open air in cold climates, but in a position where it receives the maximum sun.

N.B. This species is exceedingly variable, not only in spine count and size, but also in flower colour, ranging from yellow and orange to red and purple. The flowers are also quite large, usually exceeding 3 in (7.5 cm) in diameter.

Opuntia subterranea   *R. E. Fries*
(Argentina and Bolivia)

COLOUR: Green to dark green joints with creamy-white glochids and spines.

SIZE: Shown at slightly above natural size.

FLOWER: See Plate CCXCVII (twice natural size).

NOTE: Unlike many of the dwarf S. American Opuntias, this species is not a difficult one to flower in cultivation under glass in temperate climates.

It is not a fast growing species, possessing a well developed tap-root. The joints can vary from 1 to $1\frac{1}{2}$ in (2.5 to 3.75 cm) in length, with up to 7 short radial spines.

A sandy humus soil mixture suits this species well, and during warm weather can be given plenty of water, flowering equally well in full sun or under lightly shaded glass. In winter, a minimum temperature of 40°F (5°C) is quite sufficient, provided it is dry.

N.B. This species may also be found listed as *Tephrocactus subterraneus* Bckbg.

CEREUS GROUP

A further 24 species of plants are being included in this group, including a further nine genera—*Acanthocereus, Cephalocleistocactus, Deamia, Hildewintera, Hylocereus, Jasminocereus, Rathbunia, Selenicereus* and *Werckleocereus.*

Species of all but one of these genera are generally available today, the rarity being *Jasminocereus*, which comes from the Galapagos Islands off the coast of Ecuador in the Pacific Ocean.

Two genera, *Cephalocleistocactus* and *Hildewintera*, are relatively new to cultivation but are proving very popular because of their free-flowering qualities, particularly the latter genus, which starts flowering in very early April and continues through to the end of September, or even late October if the weather is reasonable. Both genera are propagated easily from cuttings, whilst seeds, although easy to grow, will take a number of years to reach maturity and flower.

Despite their clambering habit and quick growth, *Hylocerei* and *Selenicerei* are very popular today, particularly the former, as most species produce numerous large highly scented nocturnal flowers with the greatest of ease. Although only two species are illustrated here, most species are equally free flowering and therefore desirable.

Deamia, Rathbunia and *Werckleocereus* are also free-flowering genera. But it must be remembered that, as with the majority of *Hylocerei*, somewhat higher minimum winter temperatures are required, otherwise orange spots can develop and soon spoil a plant. This is caused by damp, cool conditions and plants can die if badly affected. *H. cubensis* is the only species we know of that winters successfully at 45°F (8°C). *Hylocereus* stock (always 3-angled) is often used as grafting stock, particularly in Japan, Germany, etc. Many amateurs lose plants that have been grafted in this way, because they do not realise that the stock is so tender, even though the scion (the plant grafted on top) would stand up to a lower temperature, if it had been on its own roots.

Acanthocereus pentagonus *B. & R.*
(Florida, Texas and N. E. Mexico)

COLOUR: Green stems with cream to black spines.
SIZE: Shown at about half natural size.
FLOWER: White flower about 8 in (20 cm) long.

NOTE: This species is exceedingly variable, in its vegetative form, from locality to locality in Florida, some forms being identical to those found in Texas and N. E. Mexico. Stems vary from 3 to 5 angled, but are usually 4, whilst the spines can vary from only ¼ in (6 mm) to nearly 2 in (5 cm) in length. The spine count varies from 4 to 9 radials and from 1 to 3 longer centrals.

It is a clambering species, freely branching with stems up to 20 ft (6.6 m) in length. In warmer countries this makes it ideal for training along dividing fences and it will produce an abundance of nicely scented nocturnal flowers. This species will grow best in a soil containing some humus with plenty of water during the spring to autumn period, less in winter and a minimum temperature of 55°F (12°C).

Cephalocleistocactus ritteri *Bckbg.*
(Bolivia)

COLOUR: Green stems almost completely obscured by the white radial spines and the golden centrals, plus fine white hairs on the flowering parts of the stems.

SIZE: Shown at just over twice natural size.

FLOWER: See Plate CCXCVIII (one and a half natural size)

NOTE: This most attractive species can grow up to 6 ft (2 m) high as can be seen in the illustration on page 1374. The stems are quite slender, only a little over 1 in (2.5. cm) in diameter, such that specimens can need a little support as and when they reach those proportions.

There can be up to 14 narrow ribs, around 30 fine white radial spines and 5 golden centrals, the longest less than $\frac{1}{2}$ in (about 1 cm) in length. Once stems reach maturity, they develop masses of quite long, fine white hairs giving the appearance of a cephalium over sections of a stem, from which flowers appear year by year.

It is of easy culture, growing in any reasonable soil, with plenty of water during the warmer growing months. In winter, it is best left dry and a minimum temperature of 40° F (5°C) is quite sufficient.

Cleistocactus dependens *Card.*
(Bolivia)

COLOUR: Green stems with brown radial spines and slightly paler centrals.

SIZE: Shown at half natural size.

FLOWER: See Plate CCXCIX.

NOTE: Although shown in the colour Plate in an erect position, this species produces very long stems which tend to clamber. However, it is certainly considered by us to be one of the freest flowering species of all and of exceedingly easy culture, particularly if given free root-run.

Stems can grow to 15 ft (5 m) or more, with up to 12 rounded ribs, 8 or more very short radial spines, and up to 4 centrals which are usually over $\frac{1}{2}$ in (1.25 cm) in length.

It will grow in any reasonable soil, with plenty of water during warm weather from spring to autumn, whilst in winter it is best left dry, when a minimum of 40°F (5°C) is quite sufficient. Our best specimen with about 5 stems produces upwards of 500 flowers each year from late March onwards into May.

This species is also known under *Seticleistocactus dependens* Bckbg.

Deamia testudo *B. & R.*
(Southern Mexico and Colombia)

COLOUR: Fresh green stems with fine golden-brown to pale brown spines.

SIZE: Shown at about natural size.

FLOWER: See Plate CCC (one-fifth natural size).

NOTE: This is an unusual clambering member of the Cereus Group, which has wing-like stems that may vary from 3 to 5 angles (occasionally more), and produces a mass of aerial roots with which to cling on to the bark of trees.

The spines are very fine, 10 or more in number per areole, and from $\frac{1}{4}$ to $\frac{1}{2}$ in (6 to 12.5 mm) in length. The flowers are diurnal, up to 12 in (30 cm) in length, also pleasantly scented.

Culture is easy, as they enjoy a soil of about 2 parts by volume of humus to 1 of gritty sand. Grown under shaded glass, with plenty of water from spring to autumn. In winter, it is safer to keep a minimum termperature of 50°F (10°C), and a little water.

Echinocereus fendleri var. bonkerae   *L. Benson*
(Arizona)

COLOUR: Green stems with short straw to cream coloured radial spines, although when new they are reddish-brown for a short time. Centrals grey with dark brown tips.

SIZE: Shown slightly larger than natural size.

FLOWER: See Plate CCCI (half natural size).

NOTE: A very beautiful, easy growing and free flowering species, which can grow into clumps of 10 or 20 heads eventually, but rarely exceeding 12 in (30 cm) in height, often much less. The rib count can vary from 11 to 16, usually less than in the *var. boyce-thompsonii*. The spine colour varies considerably, but their length is always very short, about $\frac{1}{4}$ in (6 mm).

Grows best in a soil containing at least an equal percentage of humus to gritty sand with plenty of water during the warmer months of the year. In winter, it should be left dry and is quite safe down to near freezing point.

Echinocereus gentryi *Clov.*
(Mexico)

COLOUR: Green stems with white to cream spines.

SIZE: Shown at two-thirds natural size in Plate CCCII.

FLOWER: See Plate CCCII.

NOTE: Part of a fine cluster is just visible in the illustration; the complete plant measures about 12 in (30 cm) across, the stems being about 6 in (15 cm) long and having a diameter of 1 in (2.5 cm). There are up to 12 or so very short spines per areole, one of which is termed a central.

It is exceedingly easy growing, such that any reasonable soil is suitable, with plenty of water during the spring to autumn period, when it should be grown under lightly shaded glass. In the winter, it should be left dry, when a minimum temperature of about 40°F (5°C) is preferred.

An unusual feature of this species is the fact that the flowers are open at night (and during the day if the weather is dull), but if it is hot they virtually close. There is a variety of this which is almost spineless referred to as *E. cucumis* Werd.

Echinocereus papillosus *Lke.*
(Texas)

COLOUR: Greenish stems usually tinged with pink and yellowish spines.

SIZE: Shown at three-quarters natural size in Plate CCCIII.

FLOWER: See Plate CCCIII.

NOTE: This very beautiful species is also clustering like *E. gentryi* but rather more loosely, with stems up to 12 in (30 cm) long and up to $1\frac{1}{2}$ in (3.75 cm) or more in diameter. There are around 8 spines per areole, about $\frac{1}{2}$ in (1.25 cm) long, the longest one of which is the central.

This species requires a somewhat sandy humus soil mixture, with average watering from spring to autumn, extra only if the weather is hot. Stems can become too pink tinged if in too much sun. In the winter, it should be left dry, when a minimum temperature of 40°F (5°C) is quite suitable for this species.

There is a small form of this species where the stems barely exceed 3 in (7.5 cm) in length, which goes under the name *E. papillosus var. angusticeps* Marsh, also from Texas.

Echinocereus grandis   *B. & R.*
(San Esteban and San Lorenzo Islands, Mexico)

COLOUR: Pale green body, but almost entirely obscured by the pectinate creamy to off-white coloured spines.

SIZE: Shown at just above natural size.

FLOWER: See Plate CCCIV (half natural size).

NOTE: This is normally a clustering species up to 15 in (over 40 cm) or more in height, but very erect in habit. The ribs are low, but there can be as many as 25 on a mature stem. The radial spine count can reach that number too, although often much less as the young specimen illustrated above.

It is a slow growing species, but will flower when only 3–4 in (7.5–10 cm) in height.

Culture as for *E. fendleri var. bonkerae*, but with a minimum winter temperature of 45°F (8°C).

Echinocereus melanocentrus   *Lowry*
(Texas)

COLOUR: Pale green stems, but spines can vary from white to dark brown, occasionally even a few black ones. This variability can occur from year to year, causing a sort of banding effect of the spines.

SIZE: Shown at just above natural size.

FLOWER: See Plate CCCIX (natural size).

NOTE: An exceedingly easy growing, freely clustering and exceptionally free flowering species, which up to just a few years ago was a rarity in collections.

A soil of about equal parts of gritty sand to humus is very suitable, with average water from spring to autumn, and extra in long spells of hot weather. Grows and flowers equally well under lightly shaded glass or full sun, but the latter method is only suitable for adult specimens.

In winter, if kept dry, a minimum of 40°F (5°C) or even a little lower is quite suitable. Unlike most other pectinate-spined *Echinocerei*, this species can flower in its third year from seed or even quicker when grown in more tropical climates.

Echinocereus subinermis   *Salm-Dyck*
(Mexico)

COLOUR: Bright green body with whitish areoles and creamy-yellow spines.

SIZE: Shown at a little under natural size.

FLOWER: Spiny greenish tube, petals bright yellow with prominent green stigma, flower diameter ranging from 2 to $3\frac{1}{2}$ in (5 to 8.75 cm).

NOTE: A very lovely rather soft-bodied species up to 5 in (12.5 cm) in height, solitary or branching with from 5 to 8 or 9 ribs. Areoles very small, the fine spines are very short indeed, from 4 to 8 in number.

It is an easy growing, free flowering species and flowers when young. A soil of equal parts by volume of humus and gritty sand is ideal, with average water from spring to autumn and grown under partially shaded glass. In winter, if left dry, it is quite safe down to 40°F (5°C).

Another species, *E. luteus* B. & R., also listed by Backeberg as *E. subinermis var. luteus*, is, we feel, just a form of *E. subinermis*.

Harrisia fragrans *Small*
(E. Coast of Florida)

COLOUR: Fresh green stems and grey to yellowish-brown spines appearing from the slightly woolly white areoles.

SIZE: Shown at about natural size, with a fruit only about one-third developed, but note the white hairs on it.

FLOWER: See Plate CCCVI (half natural size).

NOTE: Stems of this species can reach up to 15 ft (5 m) in length, rarely more than 2 in (5 cm) in diameter, with usually about 10 ribs, though there can be up to 12. Around 13 spines per areole, one or two of which can reach $1\frac{1}{2}$ in (3.75 cm) in length and standing out from the stems. However, these longer spines appear on older stems that have stopped growing, or on older parts of stems, these not being present in the photograph, but present in the colour plate. The fruit is about 3 in (7.5 cm) in diameter, pinkish-red when ripe.

It is of easy culture provided sufficient warmth is given, when a minimum of 50°F (10°C) is advised in winter, when it should be dry. It enjoys a soil of about equal parts by volume of humus and sand, grown under lightly shaded glass, with plenty of water during the spring to autumn period.

Harrisia simpsonii *Small*
(Florida Keys, U.S.A.)

COLOUR: Pale green stems with creamy white woolly areoles, and pale brown spines when new, changing to creamy-white.

SIZE: Shown at just over half natural size.

FLOWER: White flower up to 6 in (15 cm) long, with brownish-green outer petals, a few white hairs on the scales of the tube (Plate CCCV at a third natural size).

NOTE: Stems of this species rarely reach 9 ft (3 m) in height, but freely branching, much more so than with *H. fragrans*, about $1\frac{1}{2}$ in (3.75 cm) in diameter and usually only 9 ribs. There are usually 9 or 10 spines per areole, much shorter than with the other species, about $\frac{1}{4}$ in (6 mm) long. Fruit orange-red.

This species seems to be the freest flowering one of the trio from Florida, requiring much the same cultural treatment as *H. fragrans*, but kept a few degrees warmer in winter. Mr L. Benson refers this plant to *Cereus gracilis var. simpsonii*.

Hildewintera aureispina *Bckbg.*
Hildewintera aureispina fa. cristata *Hort.*
(Bolivia)

COLOUR: Fresh green stems partially obscured by the short, fine, brilliant golden-yellow spines.

SIZE: Shown at about two-thirds natural size.

FLOWER: See Plate CCCVII (half natural size).

NOTE: The illustration above depicts a cristate plant bearing one normal stem on the right-hand side. In order to keep a cristate plant in this weird form, all normal stems should be removed.

This is a monotypic genus; note the waxy scale-like petals around the base of the filaments of the stamens, a feature unknown in any other cactus flower—hence the erection of this separate genus.

It is a very easy plant to grow, free flowering to the extent that it will flower every year from March or April through to October. It will grow in any reasonable medium, likes plenty of root room, liberal amounts of water during the warmer months and grows and flowers equally well under lightly shaded glass or in full sun.

In winter, it should be left dry, when a minimum of 45°F (8°C) is advised. Being a somewhat pendant grower after the first few years, it will make an admirable basket-plant. It may also be seen listed under *Winteria* and *Winterocereus.*

Hylocereus cubensis *B. & R.*
(Cuba)

COLOUR: Green stems with usually an almost continuous horny greyish-brown margin and black spines.

SIZE: Shown at just under natural size.

FLOWER: See Plate CCCVIII (quarter natural size).

NOTE: The stems of this species are long and relatively slender compared with the far better known *H. undatus*. It is 3-angled, as are most normal *Hylocereus* stems. The margins can be slightly crenate, but are very distinctive because they are horny. There are 3–5 very short spines per areole.

Unlike most *Hylocerei*, this species can be grown quite safely in a greenhouse where the minimum winter temperature may fall to below 45°F (8°C). Most *Hylocerei* need a temperature above 50°F (10°C) for complete safety in winter, otherwise unsightly orange spots' can appear, sometimes sufficient to completely kill a fine specimen.

Hylocereus undatus   *B. & R.*
(Unknown)

COLOUR : Bright green stems with somewhat horny margins and straw
coloured spines.

SIZE : Shown at about one-sixth natural size.

FLOWER : Green to greenish-yellow on the outside, white within, stamens
cream coloured, highly scented.

NOTE : The stems of this species which are not shown are 3-angled, as with
H. cubensis, having markedly undulating margins. The stems are also very
long, the distance between joints varying according to climatic conditions, but
up to 3 in (7.5 cm) or more in diameter.

It is of easy culture, like *H. cubensis*, except that a minimum winter temperature of 50°F (10°C) is advised, otherwise those orange spots mentioned on
the previous page can develop.

This species was first described as *Cereus undatus* by Haworth in 1830, from
cultivated specimens sent to him from cultivation in China. Hence, the native
country of origin appearing as unknown at the top of this page.

Jasminocereus thouarsii var. sclerocarpus   *Y. Daws*
(Galapagos Islands)

COLOUR: Dark green stems, with small white areoles and white to off-white spines.

SIZE: Shown at about natural size.

FLOWER: About 2½ in (over 6 cm) in diameter, opening wide but produced on a slender tube, giving the flower a total length of over 4 in (10 cm), brownish-red in colour, with a Jasmine-like perfume.

NOTE: This is another genus which was until recently rarely seen in cultivation. But through the work of Yale Dawson in the Galapagos Islands, about fifteen years ago, some species from there are now to be seen.

It is an easy, but fairly slow growing species of eventual tree-like proportions, that is some 18 ft (6 m) in height. On older plants, one or more of the central spines can be nearly 2 in (5 cm) long. A soil of equal parts gritty sand and humus is ideal and when young the plants should be grown under lightly shaded glass, with average water for the spring to autumn period.

In winter, it should be kept dry, when a minimum of 50°F (10°C) is advised. This variety was formerly listed as a separate species, *J. sclerocarpus* Bckbg.

Lemaireocereus dumortieri *B. & R.*
(Central Mexico)

COLOUR: Pale green stems, sometimes with a powdery glaucous surface, yellowish areoles bearing yellowish-white to white spines.

SIZE: Shown at about natural size.

FLOWER: Funnel-shaped, tube scaly and spiny, brownish-red on the outside, white within, diurnal.

NOTE: Columnar-branching tree-like species up to 30 ft (10 m) in height, of easy culture and much quicker growing habit than the two species of *Pachycerei* included in this volume. The areoles are almost continuous down the acute ribs, whilst the rib count varies very little between 5 and 6.

A soil of about equal parts gritty sand and humus is ideal, with plenty of water during the spring to autumn period when it is warm. It is essential that young plants are grown under lightly shaded glass, otherwise they can burn easily. In winter, plants should be kept dry, when a minimum temperature of 45°F (8°C) is quite sufficient.

Matucana crinifera   *Ritt.*
(Peru)

COLOUR: Green body almost completely obscured by the mass of fine white spines and a few pale golden ones.

SIZE: Shown at half natural size in Plate CCCX.

FLOWER: See Plate CCCX.

NOTE: This is one of many free flowering species in this genus, but perhaps the most attractive when it comes to the beauty of the plant itself. Each areole produces up to 25 fine spines, almost hair-like bristles in many cases, some of which can be from 2 to 3 in (5 to 7.5 cm) long.

It is not a fast growing species by any means, considerably slower than *M. intertexta* shown on page 1252. A sandy humus soil mixture is required, with slightly less than average water during the growing season, unless the weather is very hot, when extra can be given. In winter, however, if dry, a minimum of 45°F (8°C) is quite sufficient, even lower if the atmospheric humidity is low.

FOOTNOTE: The longest hair-like spines do not appear until this plant reaches maturity and is within a year of flowering for the first time. Much the same thing happens with many Cleistocacti to which *Matucana* is related, in their case additional central spines appear with certain species. As young plants, they are best grown under lightly shaded glass, but once past 5 or 6 years of age this species and the other similarly spined species appreciate full sun conditions. All our specimens are grown under clear glass in a south-facing lean-to greenhouse where on occasions a shade temperature of 127°F (53°C) has been recorded!!

Matucana intertexta *Rttr.*
(Peru)

COLOUR: Fresh green body with a little white wool in the newer areoles, white radial spines, centrals off-white with brown tips.

SIZE: Shown at just under natural size.

FLOWER: See Plate CCCXI (natural size).

NOTE: This plant is of a flattened globular habit, of very easy culture and exceptionally free flowering over a two-month period here, during June and July. The flowers can vary considerably in size as well as colour, ranging from the orange shade illustrated to others which are almost a pure yellow. A little white wool can also occur on the flower tubes.

A soil of about equal parts sand and humus is ideal, with plenty of water during the spring to autumn period, when it should be grown beneath shaded glass.

In winter, if it is completely dry, it is quite safe down to 40°F (5°C).

This plant is also to be found under the generic heading *Submatucana*, a genus erected by Backeberg.

Pachycereus pecten-aboriginum *B. & R.*
(Baja California and W. coast of Mexico)

COLOUR: Dark green stems with greyish areoles and brown to grey stiff spines.

SIZE: The illustration above is shown at about two-thirds natural size.

FLOWER: Funnel-shaped, reddish outside and white within, just over 2 in (5 cm) in length, diurnal.

NOTE: Columnar branching tree-like species up to 30 ft (10 m) in height and with a basal trunk up to 18 in (40 cm) in diameter. The ribs are acute, 10–12 in number.

This species is to be found over a distance of nearly 1,600 km down the west coast of Mexico, and the further south one goes, specimens are taller but the spination is weaker. This is due to the moister conditions which prevail the further south you travel.

It is, however, a fairly slow growing species, best raised from seed rather than cuttings. Otherwise treat it as for *Lemaireocereus dumortieri*.

Pachycereus pringlei *B. & R.*
(Baja California and Sonora, Mexico)

COLOUR: Dark green stems with brown to grey woolly areoles and bearing dark brown stiff spines, later becoming grey.

SIZE: Left, one-eighth natural size; right, one-third natural size.

FLOWER: Bell-shaped, about 3 in (just over 7 cm) long, greenish-red on the outside and white within, diurnal.

NOTE: The two illustrations depict relatively young specimens (although they are far from being termed quick growers!), eventually growing into many-branched specimens up to 30 ft (10 m) high and having a basal trunk with a diameter of 3 ft (1 m) or more. The prominent rounded ribs vary from 10 to 16 in number.

In age the stems tend to lose many of their spines, in contrast to the very spiny plants which can be easily raised from seed. Cuttings are easy to root, but fortunately this is a species which is easily available in seed or seedling form.

It is quite easy to grow using a gritty sand and humus mixture in about equal parts; average water and grown under lightly shaded glass for the first three or four years. After that, full sun conditions are preferred in order to develop the strong spination. In winter, plants should be left dry, when a temperature down to 40°F (5°C) is sufficient.

Rathbunia alamosensis fa. cristata *Hort.*
(Mexico)

COLOUR: Fresh green stems with white radial spines and grey to grey-brown centrals on the normal plant illustrated on page 1256. The cristate form above tends in sun to become pinkish-brown towards the upper new growth regions, whilst the fine juvenile spines are off-white to golden-brown.

SIZE: Shown at about natural size in both cases.

FLOWER: See Plate CCCXII.

NOTE: A very easy growing species no matter whether it is in the normal or cristate form. The normal form shown overleaf can grow into a somewhat straggling bush in height up to 12 ft (4 m), usually much less, whilst the cristate form grows into a mound.

It will grow in any reasonable soil, with plenty of water from spring to autumn; it grows best under lightly shaded glass, and has a flowering period which lasts for a month or so.

In winter, however, plants can be left dry, when a minimum temperature of 50°F (10°C) is required; otherwise at lower temperatures, particularly if the atmospheric humidity is fairly high, plants can become disfigured by orange marks. In some cases it can kill them completely.

Rathbunia alamosensis   *B. & R.*

This is the form of the normal plant.

Rathbunia kerberi   *B. & R.*
(Mexico)

COLOUR: Fresh green stems, a little grey wool on the areoles, off-white radial spines, grey centrals which are not flattened as with *R. alamosensis*, annular rings not so prominent.

SIZE: Shown at about two-thirds natural size.

FLOWER: 4½ in (12 cm) long, rose-red in colour, somewhat zygomorphic. See Plate CCCXIII for habitat illustration of a 6 ft (2 m) high plant, filmed on the Pacific coast of Mexico near Mazatlan.

NOTE: Unlike *R. alamosensis*, which normally has 5 rounded ribs, this species has 4, giving the stems a much squarer appearance. It is also much more erect in habit, as can be seen by the habitat illustration of an adult plant in Plate CCCXIII.

It requires identical soil and growing conditions as *R. alamosensis*, but in winter a slightly higher minimum temperature is advised, otherwise those disfiguring blotches can appear.

Selenicereus grandiflorus *B. & R.*
(Jamaica and Cuba)

COLOUR: Green stems with yellowish-brown spines.

SIZE: Shown at about two-thirds natural size.

FLOWER: See Plate CCCXIV (one-quarter natural size).

NOTE: This is a very lovely species as you can see by the colour illustration of the 12–14 in (30–35 cm) diameter flower. As with most members of this genus it is not only easy to grow, but flowers freely during the late spring on to mid-summer.

The 7- to 8-angled stems rarely exceed 1 in (2.5 cm) in diameter, but grow to immense lengths, freely branching and producing a mass of aerial roots, which are used for clinging on to trees and cliffs as well as for obtaining nourishment.

This species, like most others, will grow in any reasonable soil, with plenty of water during the spring to autumn period. They should be grown under shaded glass, otherwise stems can easily burn.

In winter, however, a minimum temperature of 45°F (8°C) is sufficient if kept dry and the atmospheric humidity is low. A few degrees higher is better for all the known species, then there is no risk of damage from 'orange spots'.

Selenicereus urbanianus *B. & R.*
(Haiti and Cuba)

COLOUR: Dull green stems sometimes tinged with purplish-brown if in sun, and brownish spines.

SIZE: Shown at half natural size in Plate CCCXV.

FLOWER: See Plate CCCXV.

NOTE: Although the flowers of this species are somewhat smaller than those of *S. grandiflorus*, being usually no more than 10 in (25 cm) in length and a diameter of 6 in (15 cm), it is not only very free flowering, but also the first species in the genus to flower each year.

The stems are 4- or 5-angled usually, with small white areoles and a few short fine brown spines, let alone numerous aerial roots which are common to this genus.

This species copes with full sun conditions far better than most others, grows in any reasonable soil, and likes plenty of water during the spring to autumn period. This species, if dry in winter, is quite safe down to 45°F (8°C) or even lower without any harm being done.

WErckleocereus tonduzii *B. & R.*
(Costa Rica)

COLOUR: Green to brownish-green stems and small off-white areoles without spines.

SIZE: Shown at half natural size in Plate CCCXVI.

FLOWER: See Plate CCCXVI.

NOTE: This is usually a 3-angled stemmed species, somewhat like *Hylocereus*, to which it is related, and producing aerial roots in the same way. Although the stems are usually spineless, the flower tube has black wool and clusters of short black spines.

It is of easy culture, enjoying a soil with a fairly high proportion of humus, plenty of water from spring to autumn, when it should be grown under partially shaded glass. In winter, assuming it is not in too small a pot or has free root-run, it can be left quite dry, when a minimum of 50°F (10°C) is sufficient.

Unlike many *Hylocerei*, this species is quite suitable for the person with a small greenhouse.

PILOCEREUS GROUP

In this volume we are introducing a further four genera which will be new to this group—*Arrojadoa, Austrocephalocereus, Haageocereus* and *Stephanocereus*—as well as bringing in the generic name *Pilosocereus* for many of the species previously described as *Cephalocereus*.

The interesting point with some of these genera is the way in which the cephalium or pseudocephalium varies from a lateral to a terminal form and how those genera with terminal ones grow through it and then repeat the process.

The *Haageocereus acranthus*, which is illustrated, was grown from seed collected by the late Curt Backeberg and took some forty years to reach flowering size. During the war years (1939–1945) and for a few years afterwards, plants were forced to remain in small pots for too long. But for this, it would probably have flowered at least ten years earlier. The stems which are now appearing from the base of the original double-stemmed plant are now growing far more rapidly than previously.

Pilosocereus keyensis, or *Cephalocereus keyensis* as it was formerly known, had fascinated us for a very long time—along with *Cephalocereus deeringii*—as, despite their home being Florida, they were never seen in cultivation. In 1973, one of our trips was in search of the cacti of Florida, which are so poorly known today. Brian Lamb joined up with a very good friend and horticulturist, Pete Forrester, determined to either find one or both of these species on the Keys (in the south of Florida) or prove that they are extinct in habitat. They are certainly very rare in habitat, as are the native Harrisias, and we are still not certain whether '*deeringii*' does exist as its original type locality has been completely wiped out. We did, however, find a few specimens not too far from the type locality, but they do not match the description of '*deeringii*' very closely.

Arrojadoa penicillata   *B. & R.*
(Brazil)

COLOUR: Green stems with grey-brown spines with much finer brown bristle type spines on the terminal pseudocephalium.

SIZE: Shown at about half natural size.

FLOWER: See Plate CCCXVII (2½ times natural size).

NOTE: This species will flower when only 6 in (15 cm) high and even in age stems only reach 3–6 ft (1–2 m).

The stems which rarely exceed ½ in (1.25 cm) in diameter have about 10 ribs, areoles small and set very close together bearing up to 14 spines of which 1 or 2 are centrals. The longest can sometimes be as much as 1 in (2.5 cm), somewhat shorter on the specimen illustrated.

As one can see, the pseudocephalium is terminal. The plant may flower from it for two or three years before the stem grows on through it, and repeats the process.

A soil of about equal parts humus and sand and plenty of water during the spring to autumn period is suitable under lightly shaded glass, with a minimum winter temperature of 50° (10°C), when it should be kept dry.

Arrojadoa rhodantha *B. & R.*
(Brazil)

COLOUR: Fresh green stems with golden-brown spines.

SIZE: Shown at about natural size.

FLOWER: Similar to that of the previous species, *A. penicillata*, pink in colour but up to 1½ in (3.75 cm) long.

NOTE: This plant has a very similar habit to that of *A. penicillata*, growing up to 6 ft (2 m) in height but having much stouter and more rigid stems up to 1½ in (3.75 cm) or more in diameter. The rib count ranges from 10 to 14, whilst there can be up to 20 radial spines and 6 centrals, the longest of which rarely exceeds 1 in (2.5 cm) in length, mostly much less.

The terminal pseudocephalium is made up of wool and masses of very fine golden-brown spines, quite different to those on the stems.

Cultivation requirements are the same as those for *A. penicillata*.

Austrocephalocereus dybowskii *Bckbg.*
(Brazil)

COLOUR: Green body almost completely obscured by the very dense covering of white hairs and golden-yellow spines. The lateral pseudocephalium is a mass of pure white wool.

SIZE: Shown (top of a stem) at about one-third natural size.

FLOWER: The nocturnal flowers are 1½ in (4 cm) long, white to pale pink.

NOTE: Even before the pseudocephalium appears and flowering commences, these are most attractive plants, a little similar to *Espostoa* in general appearance. Stems branch at the base and can reach a height of 6–12 ft (2–4 m). The only visible spines are the 2 or 3 centrals per areole, which can reach up to 1 in (2.5 cm) in length.

Not fast growing, but not unduly difficult to grow, given a soil of about equal parts humus and gritty sand, average watering during warm weather. During dull cool weather, plants are best left dry; in winter a minimum temperature of 50°F (10°C) is advised, when they should be left dry.

Formerly known as *Cephalocereus dybowskii* Goss., whilst Buxbaum lists it under *Espostoopsis*.

Haageocereus acranthus   *Bckbg.*
(Peru)

COLOUR: Green stems with yellowish-brown to brown spines.

SIZE: Shown at about half natural size.

FLOWER: See Plate CCCXVIII (1½ times natural size).

NOTE: This species branches freely from the base with erect stems up to 6–9 ft (2–3 m) in height, and around 2½–3 in (6.25–7.5 cm) in diameter. There are 12–14 low ribs, bearing large felted and spiny areoles. There can be from 20 to 30 radial spines, the longest no more than ⅜ in (1.0 cm), whilst the centrals (1 or 2) can range from 1 to 2 in (2.5 to 5 cm) in length.

It is a slow growing species, which will take many years to reach maturity and flower, but worth growing just for the plant's appearance. It enjoys a soil of about equal parts humus and sand, with average watering from spring to autumn. For its first few years from seed it should be grown under lightly shaded glass, but from then on enjoys full sun. In winter, provided it is kept dry, it is quite safe down to 40°F (5°C).

If this plant can be given free root-run conditions after the first four or five years, much better results will be obtained.

Pilosocereus keyensis *Byles & Rowley*
(Florida)

COLOUR: Green to yellowish-green stems, with small white woolly areoles and golden-yellow spines that fade to off-white or grey with age.

SIZE: Shown at about natural size.

FLOWER: Brownish-purple in colour, campanulate, about $2\frac{1}{2}$ in (just over 6 cm) long and with a garlic scent (Plate CCCXIX).

NOTE: This species can reach up to 18 ft (6 m) or so in height, but is not freely branching. Plate CCCXIX depicts a specimen of similar proportions. It has 9 or 10 ribs, whilst the areoles produce from 12 to 16 fine spines in varying lengths, the longest being just over $\frac{1}{2}$ in (1.25 cm).

It requires a soil of about 2 parts by volume of humus to 1 of gritty sand, plenty of water during the warmer growing months, under lightly shaded glass. In winter, it can be left dry, when a minimum of 50°F (10°C) is required.

This was formerly known as *Cephalocereus keyensis* B. & R., whilst today some authorities classify this as a synonym of *Cephalocereus robinii* Lem. from Cuba, a quite different multi-branched tree with a very thick basal trunk.

Pilosocereus lanuginosus *Byles & Rowley*
(Netherlands Antilles and Venezuela)

COLOUR: Pale bluish-green stems with white areoles, the newer ones containing a lot of long white hairs. Spines when new yellowish, changing to off-white.

SIZE: Shown (top of a stem) at about half natural size.

FLOWER: Flowers appear from amid the white wooly pseudocephalium, 2 in (5 cm) long, greeny-cream colour on the outside of the petals and varying shades of pink on the inside (Plate CCCXX). The colour illustration on page 1382 depicts a 6 ft (2 m) high specimen just starting to produce the white woolly pseudo-cephalium; this was filmed by us in Curacao.

NOTE: Columnar, branching tree-like species up to 24 ft (8 m) in height, but such specimens will be many years old. It is an easy growing species which will grow in any reasonable soil, enjoys plenty of water during the warmer months of the year and if it can be given a free root-run, then much quicker growth will be obtained.

Culture as for *P. keyensis.* This species was formerly listed as *Cephalocereus lanuginosus* B. & R.

Stephanocereus leucostele *Berg.*
(Brazil)

COLOUR: Green body almost obscured by the white hair and spines, whilst the terminal cephalium is made up of white wool and bristles.

SIZE: Shown at about half natural size.

FLOWER: Somewhat tubular, greenish, just under 3 in (about 7 cm) long.

NOTE: This species is usually solitary, varying from 6 to 15 ft (2 to 5 m) in height, with up to 18 low ribs, whilst the spine count per areole can vary a great deal, the longest ones being up to 2 in (5 cm).

As with *Arrojadoa*, the stem will grow on through the terminal cephalium and will later produce another one, and another and so on. Like *Arrojadoas* and *Oreocereus doelzianus* (sometimes referred to as *Morawetzia doelziana Bckbg.*), flowers will often appear from the collar remains of the cephalium as well as from the new terminal one.

A humus and sand mixture of about equal parts suits this species well, with average water during the warmer months, less or none when cool. In winter, it should be kept dry, when a minimum of 50°F (10°C) is required.

This species was formerly known as *Cephalocereus leucostele* Gurke.

ECHINOPSIS GROUP

In this volume, one *Acanthocalycium* and also a single species of *Lobivia* are included in this group. However, a further three *Rebutias* are being included, as well as introducing for the first time by name the genus *Sulcorebutia*. This genus, in the last ten years or so, has become exceptionally popular—to such an extent that we have included seven of them.

As a general rule, in this fifth volume, we have included, where it was necessary, close-up colour photographs to add to the half-tone close-ups of the plant. In this instance, however, as the plants are all generally clumping kinds of dwarf habit, some species are being shown in colour only, as sufficient plant detail is available in these instances.

Certain modifications in the nomenclature of the genus *Rebutia* have been made, such that in the listing of species in the previous volumes name changes appear in brackets. One of these is *Rebutia steinbachii*, appeared in Volume IV and is now referred to as *Sulcorebutia steinbachii* Bckbg.

There has been considerable controversy over *Sulcorebutia* versus *Rebutia*, particularly as in present-day thinking certain generic names are disappearing as species are transferred into other closely related genera, thus reducing the number of genera. However, following the I.O.S. working party on the taxonomic relationships within the genus *Rebutia* K. Sch., it was unanimously decided that *Sulcorebutias* should not be included within the genus *Rebutia*. This was based on a system of important characteristics of the plant from rib structure, areole position, flower and fruit, similar to that described in an article by Gordon Rowley in an issue of the *Cactus and Succulent Journal of America* in 1967 headed 'Cactus and the Computer'. Although *Sulcorebutia* in general appearance seems very close to *Rebutia* it was discovered that it was almost equally related to *Lobivia* and *Weingartia*, rather than to *Rebutia*.

Acanthocalycium glaucum *Rttr.*
(Argentina)

COLOUR: Bluish-green to slate-grey body colour, with white wool on the newer areoles. Spines dark brown when new, changing to greyish-brown or grey later.

SIZE: Shown at just above natural size.

FLOWER: See Plate CCCXXII (one-third natural size).

NOTE: A very lovely solitary globular to slightly columnar species which can reach 6 in (15 cm) in height and have up to 14 straight ribs. There are up to 8 or more radial spines, centrals rarely present, average spine length just under 1 in (2.5 cm).

Note in the colour plate how the flower can vary considerably from one plant to another, their average diameter being around $2\frac{1}{2}$ in (6.25 cm).

It is not a quick growing species, but grows well in a humus and sand mixture of about equal parts, with average watering during the spring to autumn period. This is quite a tough bodied species which, once past the seedling stage, can take full sun conditions. In winter, if left dry they are quite safe down to 40°F (5°C), or even a little lower.

Lobivia hualfinensis var. fechseri *Rausch.*
(N. Argentina)

COLOUR: Green body sometimes tinged with a pinkish-bronze and pink-ish-grey spines, changing to grey with age.

SIZE: Shown at nearly one and a half times natural size.

FLOWER: See Plate CCCXXIII (half natural size).

NOTE: This is a very lovely small growing species, solitary or sparingly clustering but very free flowering and these ranging in colour as can be seen on the colour illustration.

Unlike many cacti, the rib count is very constant at 10, whilst the 1 in (2.5 cm) long spines, sometimes a little less, vary from 7 to 10 per areole, of which 1 may be present as a central, standing straight out from the plant.

Cultivation is very easy with this fairly new species, using a soil of equal parts gritty sand and humus, plenty of water during the spring to autumn period when it is essential that it is grown under lightly shaded glass. In winter, if dry, it is quite safe down to 40°F (5°C).

Rebutia muscula *Ritt. & Thiel.*
(Bolivia)

COLOUR: Green body almost completely obscured by the white spines.

SIZE: Shown at about one-third above natural size.

FLOWER: See Plate CCCXXIV (half natural size).

NOTE: This must be one of the finest new introductions in recent years in this genus, capable of flowering over a long period during the spring and early summer, and again in the late autumn.

It forms into quite large clumps eventually, heads eventually reaching a height of 2 in (5 cm) and having a diameter of about 1½ in (3.75 cm), even when grown on its own roots.

It grows well in a soil of about equal parts humus and sand under lightly shaded glass with plenty of water during the spring to autumn period. In winter, it can be left dry, when a minimum temperature of 40°F (5°C) is quite sufficient.

FOOTNOTE: Do not confuse with the small red-flowered *R. minuscula* Sch.

Rebutia pulvinosa   *Ritt. & Buin*
(Bolivia)

COLOUR: Green body and off-white spines.

SIZE: Shown at slightly above natural size.

FLOWER: Orange coloured.

NOTE: This is another fairly new free flowering species, possessing relatively slender stems up to 2 in (5 cm) in height and only around ¾ in (about 2 cm) in diameter. Each areole carries up to 14 or so very fine spines in varying lengths.

It is not as fast a growing species as *R. muscula*, but its cultural requirements are much the same.

Sulcorebutia breviflora   *Bckbg.*
(Bolivia)

COLOUR: Green body partially obscured by the off-white to light brown spines.

SIZE: Shown at just above natural size.

FLOWER: Golden-yellow.

NOTE: A most attractive species, very free flowering and grows into quite large clumps, with the heads reaching a diameter of around 2 in (5 cm). The quite prominent creamy coloured areoles produce up 12 or more fine spines, the longest of which can be nearly $\frac{1}{2}$ in (1.25 cm).

This particular species comes from an altitude of around 6,000 ft (2,000 m), whereas some other species are to be found much higher up, such as *Sulcorebutia glomerispina* which comes from over 9,000 ft (3,000 m). Cultural requirements as for *R. muscula*.

Sulcorebutia breviflora has also been listed under *Rebutia brachyantha* Card.

Sulcorebutia rauschii *Frank*
(Bolivia)

COLOUR: Dark green body heavily blotched with purple, with purple-black spines.

SIZE: Shown at about two-thirds natural size.

FLOWER: See Plate CCCXXVII (1½ times natural size).

NOTE: This is a most unusual but very attractive species, even without its magenta-pink flowers, due to the plant being so highly coloured. There are up to 10 very short dark spines per areole completely flattened against the plant body, each head of which can sometimes be as much as 1½ in (3.75 cm) in diameter.

The specimen illustrated above is another of our demonstration grafts and it is interesting to note that one head on this plant is becoming cristate.

Cultural requirements are as for *R. muscula.*

Rebutia eos *Lau*
(Bolivia)

COLOUR: Dull green body and glassy white to cream spines.

SIZE: Shown at two-thirds natural size in Plate CCCXXV.

FLOWER: See Plate CCCXXV.

NOTE: This is quite a new species and is related to such species as *R. haagei* and *R. pygmaea*, which have a very similar stem formation and were once listed under *Mediolobivia*. The older stems can reach a height of 2 in (5 cm) and about 1 in (25 mm) in diameter, whilst each areole has from 8 to 12 very fine short spines, which are completely flattened against the plant.

As with its relatives, it develops quite a succulent root system and forms eventually into quite large flat but very dense clumps.

Cultural requirements are as for *R. muscula*.

Sulcorebutia alba *Rausch.*
(Bolivia)

COLOUR: Green body almost obscured by the white spines.

SIZE: Shown at 1¼ times natural size in Plate CCCXXI.

FLOWER: See Plate CCCXXI.

NOTE: A very distinctive tightly clustering species, with the heads varying from 1 to 1½ in (2.5 to 3.75 cm) in diameter. There are up to 18 short spines per areole, which are also flattened against the plant body.

Cultivation requirements as for *R. muscula*.

Sulcorebutia caniqueralii   *Bckbg.*
(Bolivia)

COLOUR: Green to pale green body with purplish-brown spines that change to a horny colour towards the tips.

SIZE: Shown at 1½ times natural size in Plate CCCXXVI.

FLOWER: See Plate CCCXXVI.

NOTE: This beautiful bicoloured species flowers very freely during the spring and early summer. It is tightly clustering, the heads only just exceeding 1 in (2.5 cm) in diameter with up to 14 short fine spines flattened against the body of the plant.

This species was originally described by Professor Cardenas in 1964 under *Rebutia caniqueralii.*

Cultivation requirements as for *R. muscula.*

Sulcorebutia kruegeri   *Ritt.*
(Bolivia)

COLOUR: Dark green body with off-white to golden-brown spines.

SIZE: Shown at one-third natural size in Plate CCCXXXIII.

FLOWER: See Plate CCCXXXIII.

NOTE: This is a strong growing species no matter whether it is on its own roots or grafted, with heads often exceeding 1½ in (3.75 cm) in diameter. The prominently elongated areoles produce up to 20 fine curved spines, somewhat flattened against the plant.

This was originally described by Professor Cardenas as *Aylostera kruegeri.*

Cultivation requirements as for *R. muscula.*

Sulcorebutia lepida *Ritt.*
(Bolivia)

COLOUR: Dark green body with reddish-brown spines.

SIZE: Shown at 1½ times natural size in Plate CCCXXVIII.

FLOWER: See Plate CCCXXVIII.

NOTE: This very distinctive species, originally described in 1962, clusters rather more slowly than some species. A mature head can reach a diameter of 1½ in (3.75 cm), each areole producing up to 20 curved spines, 3 of which are considerably longer.

Cultural requirements as for *R. muscula.*

Sulcorebutia tiraquensis *Bckbg.*
(Bolivia)

COLOUR: Dark green body with white and dark brown spines.

SIZE: Shown at 1¼ times natural size in Plate CCCXXIX.

FLOWER: See Plate CCCXXIX.

NOTE: This is a most attractive species, often remaining solitary for many years, such that it can reach a diameter of 2½ in (6.25 cm). There are usually around 21 spines, mostly fine but up to 3 of these are much stiffer and can be anything from ½ to 1 in (1.25–2.5 cm) long.

This species and its varieties are somewhat slower growing, but can be expected to flower very freely each year. Cultural requirements as for *R. muscula.*

This species was originally described in 1958 by Professor Cardenas as *Rebutia tiraquensis.*

ECHINOCACTUS GROUP

In the previous four volumes over 130 species from 35 genera have already been included from this group. We now add a further 28 species, which will also introduce a further 3 genera—*Islaya, Oroya Uebelmannia,* the first two from Peru, the *Uebelmannia* from Brazil. It is only in the last decade that *Islaya* and *Oroya* have become more generally available, whilst *Uebelmannia* is still relatively uncommon in cultivation.

In the previous volumes, various *Ferocacti* have been illustrated, mostly as relatively young plants, and such plants differ considerably in rib count from those specimens of more mature years. It is important to remember when checking a botanical description to take this into account. It is for this reason that we are including some colour habitat illustrations of *F. emoryi* and *F. stainesii,* in addition to the half-tones of smaller specimens in our collection of *F. herrerae* and *F. stainesii.*

One of the Gymnocalyciums included, *G. ragonesii,* is shown alongside a British 1p coin (just over $\frac{3}{4}$ in or about 2 cm in diameter). It is certainly one of the finest miniatures in that genus, capable of flowering each year over a period of three or four months.

COLOUR PLATES
Illustrated in Volume IV

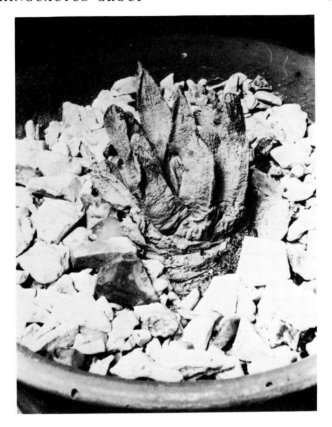

Ariocarpus scapharostrus *Bdkr.*
(Mexico)

COLOUR: The triangular tubercles have a rough surface, which is of a chalky to slate-grey colour.

SIZE: Shown at slightly above natural size.

FLOWER: Just under 2 in (5 cm) in diameter, magenta.

NOTE: A dwarf growing species, which can eventually reach a diameter of 3½ in (8.25 cm). Exceedingly slow growing and requiring a very porous soil, and one which should always be grown in a clay pot—never plastic! A soil containing about 2 parts by volume of grit and sand to 1 humus is quite suitable, with less than average water at all times.

In winter, it must be kept completely dry, when it is quite safe down to a minimum of 40°F (5°C). In its native habitat it endures extremes, growing on completely barren hillsides amongst rocks and mica, where temperatures are exceptionally high in summer and also quite chilly in winter, but always very dry.

Blossfeldia fechseri *Bckbg.*
(Argentina)

COLOUR: Olive-green body tending to become grey with age, white areoles.

SIZE: Shown at nearly one and a half times natural size.

FLOWER: Creamy-white on the inside but reddish-purple on the exterior of the petals and the base of the flower.

NOTE: In Volume III (page 648) we illustrated the type species for the genus, *Blossfeldia liliputana*. *B. fechseri* is named after H. Fechser who has carried out a lot of exploration work in Argentina.

B. fechseri has heads about twice the size of *B. liliputana*, larger and more colourful flowers, which appear over many months from late spring onwards.

It is not a difficult species to grow on its own roots, although it is very slow indeed to cluster to any extent. It needs a sandy humus soil mixture, grown under shaded glass (this is very important to prevent burning that will cause heads to dry up completely) and plenty of mist spraying even between normal applications of water. In winter, a minimum temperature of 45°F (8°C) is sufficient, when they should be kept dry. If the weather is very mild at that time of year an occasional mist spraying will be beneficial.

Copiapoa hypogaea *Ritt.*
(Chile)

COLOUR: Greyish-brown to slate coloured body with white wool in the centre, also in the older areoles, and brownish spines.

SIZE: Shown at just under one and a half times natural size.

FLOWER: About 1½ in (3.75 cm) in diameter, lemon-yellow, opening very wide.

NOTE: This is one of the smaller growing species, sometimes remaining solitary but occasionally branching a little, of slightly flattened globular habit.

It is very free flowering from mid-summer until the late autumn. It is, however, a relatively slow growing species, requiring a sandy humus soil mixture, about average watering, growing and flowering equally well under lightly shaded glass or in full sun. In winter, it should be kept dry, when a minimum temperature of 40°F (5°C) is quite sufficient.

Copiapoa rupestris   *Rttr.*
(Chile)

COLOUR: Chalky-green body, tending to darken with age, areoles having a little white wool, whilst the new spines in the centre of the plant are black. These change gradually to white at the bases, but greyer towards the tips. Old spines nearer the bottom of a plant change to a dirty brown colour.

SIZE: Shown at about natural size.

FLOWER: Flower similar in structure to that of *C. hypogaea*, usually a darker yellow colour, but not so free flowering.

NOTE: A slow growing, flattened globular species possessing a long and very succulent tap-root. A very distinctive species, but sadly a shy flowerer until specimens are quite large.

It requires a sandy humus growing mixture, a deep pot to accommodate its lengthy tap-root, and less than average water—although extra water is safe in long spells of hot weather. This species grows best under full sun conditions, once plants are well passed the seedling stage.

In winter, a minimum temperature of 40°F (5°C) is quite sufficient, provided it is kept dry. Under conditions of low atmospheric humidity even low temperatures are quite safe.

Echinocactus polycephalus *Engelm. & Big.*
(S.W. U.S.A. and N. Mexico)

COLOUR: Grey-green body with pinkish-grey to bright pink spines, changing to shades of brown with age.

SIZE: Shown at about one-quarter natural size.

FLOWER: Yellow and just over 2 in (5 cm) in diameter.

NOTE: This is very slow growing, usually remaining solitary for many years, but eventually sprouting from the base to form large groups. The heads can reach nearly 3 ft (1 m) in height and up to 1 ft (30 cm) in diameter.

The body of the plant is very hard indeed, as are the spines. There are usually 4 central spines, flattened and with annular rings, the longest up to nearly 4 in (10 cm) in length.

It requires a well drained growing medium, with slightly less than average water at all times. Once passed the seedling stage, it appreciates full sun conditions. In winter if dry, it can stand very cool conditions as some of the more northerly forms in habitat endure below freezing temperatures. However, in damper climates a winter minimum of 40°F (5°C) is safer.

Ferocactus emoryi *Bckbg.*
(N. W. Mexico)

COLOUR: Green body becoming greyish with age as the base becomes woody, spines golden-yellow to pink.

SIZE: Shown at one-thirtieth natural size in Plate CCCXXX.

FLOWER: Usually over 2 in (5 cm) long, gold to golden-red'

NOTE: In this instance we show only a very old plant just over 6 ft (2 m) high filmed by us in habitat near Guaymas, Sonora, during June 1976. This species has been recorded at over 7 ft (2.3 m) in height.

Once this species starts to become columnar, it can have from 22 to 32 ribs; these are quite high and angular up to as much as 2 in (5 cm). The areoles, which are somewhat woolly when new, produce from 5 to 8 radial spines and 1 curved central.

In cultivation, as with most *Ferocacti*, a soil of about equal parts gritty sand and humus is needed, with average water for the spring to autumn period. Best growth is obtained in a wide but relatively shallow pan. In winter, a minimum of 45°F (8°C) is preferable, when plants should be left completely dry. Young plants need to be grown under lightly shaded glass, whereas older specimens upwards of ten years can take full sun.

Ferocactus stainesii *B. & R.*
(Mexico)

COLOUR: Green body, white areoles in the newer growth, white radial hairs, spines reddish.

SIZE: Shown at one-third natural size in illustration overleaf.

FLOWER: Usually over 2 in (5 cm) long, orange to orange-red.

NOTE: This is a very well known species, which in age can cluster as can be seen in Plate CCCXXXI showing a specimen where the main head is about 4½ ft (1.5 m) high. A close-up of one head with ripe fruit is shown in Plate CCCXXXII.

On a more mature plant than the one shown on the next page, there can be from 18 to 20 quite narrow ribs, each areole producing 3 or 4 and even as many as 12 fine radial hair-like spines, plus 8 or 9 other very stout spines. The flattened ones can be termed centrals, one of these being much longer than the rest, wider and up to 2 in (5 cm) long.

Cultural requirements as for *F. emoryi*.

FOOTNOTE: The relatively young non-flowering specimen overleaf has only a few of the fine white radial hair-like spines. However, once near flowering size these will increase considerably and are then clearly visible. This species is somewhat similar to *F. pringlei*. B. & R., listed by Backeberg as *F. stainesii* var. *pringlei*. Bckbg. The ribs of *F. pringlei* are set somewhat closer together, as are the areoles, and has a larger number of spines per areole, also

Ferocactus stainesii (young specimen)

can grow up to 9 ft (3 m) in height, often forming into quite massive groups.
Two other varieties are also listed under *F. stainesii*, these are *F. stainesii* var.
haematacanthus. Bckbg. and *F. stainesii* var. *pilosus*. Bckbg.

Ferocactus herrerae   *G. Ort.*
(Mexico)

COLOUR: Dark green body giving a slightly shiny appearance, with white wool at the newer areoles, whilst the spines are in varying shades of red, but these pale to pinkish-brown or grey-brown with age.

SIZE: Shown at about half natural size.

FLOWER: Orange-red in colour, about 3 in (7.5 cm) in diameter.

NOTE: A very attractive species, particularly as it gets older, due to the much heavier spination it produces.

It is normally solitary and can eventually grow up to 6 ft (2m) in height. Adult plants have 13–14 ribs, whereas the plant illustrated above is only just starting to change from its tubercled appearance, which is common to all young *Echinocacti* and *Ferocacti*. On old specimens annular rings appear on one or more of the central spines.

Cultural requirements as for *F. emoryi*.

Gymnocalycium horstii *Buin.*
(Brazil)

COLOUR: Bright green body with cream to almost yellowish wool in the areoles and cream coloured spines.

SIZE: Shown at about one-half natural size.

FLOWER: See Plate CCCXXXIV (two-thirds natural size).

NOTE: This very beautiful *Gymnocalycium* was discovered by the late A. F. H. Buining, and described by him in 1970. It is similar to *G. denudatum* illustrated in Volume I (page 108). However, that species is more depressed in its body form, and has a dry fruit, let alone floral differences.

The flowers of *G. horstii* may last for up to a week, varying in colour from pale tangerine to pink, but gradually fading.

It clusters very freely, flowers over six to eight weeks during mid-summer and grows well in a humus and gritty sand soil mixture of about equal parts with plenty of water during all warm weather. It grows best under lightly shaded glass, whilst in winter, if dry, a minimum temperature of 45°F (8°C) is required.

Gymnocalycium ragonesii   *Cast.*
(Bolivia)

COLOUR: Brownish-green to slate-coloured body with whitish spines.

SIZE: The 1p coin shown with these two plants measures just over ¾ in (2 cm) in diameter.

FLOWER: Pure white flower just exceeding 1½ in (3.75 cm) in length.

NOTE: This is a quite fabulous little miniature, which can eventually only grow up to 2 in (5 cm) or so in diameter. Even with the slower growth rate in the British climate, it can be flowered in eighteen months from seed!! The flowering period often extends over three months or more, from late spring onwards.

A mixture of equal parts gritty sand and humus suits this species very well, with average water and grown under lightly shaded glass. In winter if kept dry it is quite safe down to 45°F (8°C). It does have a very flat habit and during the dry winter months it will tend to pull itself down level with the soil or grit.

Hamatocactus uncinatus var. wrightii   *Engelm. ex Borg.*
(Texas and Mexico)

COLOUR: Bluish-green body, off-white to grey radial spines, whilst the long centrals tend to be much darker coloured, although they pale with age.

SIZE: Shown at about one-third natural size.

FLOWER: See Plate CCCXXXV (1½ times natural size).

NOTE: A solitary columnar growing plant which can grow up to 8 in (20 cm) or so in height without accounting for the 6 in (15 cm) long central spines.

This variety needs a much better drained soil and less than average water, growing best under lightly shaded glass.

In winter, it should be kept completely dry, when a minimum of 40°F (5°C) is sufficient, although if the atmospheric humidity is high a higher temperature will be safer. In habitat, at some of the locations in Texas, it does cope safely with temperatures below freezing point, but under quite dry conditions and often under the protection of some xerophytic bush.

It has been listed under *Echinocactus, Echinomastus, Glandulicactus* and *Thelocactus.*

Islaya bicolor *Akers & Buin.*
(S. Peru)

COLOUR: Grey-green to almost chalky-green body, sometimes tinged with pink, spines pinkish-brown when new, becoming grey with age.

SIZE: Shown at nearly one and a half times natural size.

FLOWER: Satin-yellow tinged with red towards tips of petals, less than 1 in (2.5 cm) in height and diameter.

NOTE: This species becomes somewhat columnar in age but rarely exceeds 7 in (17.5 cm) or so in height, with a maximum diameter of 4 in (10 cm). There can be around 14–16 ribs, often slightly spiralled and somewhat notched such that the off-white woolly areoles are slightly raised. There can be from 10 to 14 or so radial spines and usually 4 centrals, the longest being just over ½ in (1.25 cm) all of them very rigid.

This genus is related to *Notocactus*, but in contrast to their easy culture, all members of this genus need more care. They require a very well drained soil of about 2 parts by volume of gritty sand to 1 of humus, less than average water and top shelf position in the greenhouse. Once beyond their first two or three years, they can take full sun conditions, but flower equally well under lightly shaded glass. In winter, a minimum of 45°F (8°C) is required with completely dry conditions.

Islaya divaricatiflora *Ritt.*
(Peru)

COLOUR: Pale green body tending to become grey and corky nearer soil level. Spines gingery when new, later becoming grey.

SIZE: Shown at slightly above natural size.

FLOWER: Greenish-yellow petals tinged with red towards their tips.

NOTE: This is a much smaller growing species than *I. bicolor*, but its diameter can in age sometimes reach nearly 3 in (7.5 cm) at the base. There are 16 ribs on this fairly young but flowering size specimen, but this can increase eventually to as much as 25. These ribs again can be slightly spiralled with raised areoles and 12 or more very short radial spines plus anything from 3 to 8 centrals, the longest of which is only $\frac{1}{4}$ in (6 mm).

Cultivation requirements are the same as for *I. bicolor*.

Islaya krainziana *Ritt.*
(N. Chile and S. Peru)

COLOUR: Dark grey-green body, creamy-white wool in the areoles and the spines are dark reddish-brown in the centre changing to grey with age, but shading to grey-black towards their tips.

SIZE: Shown at just above natural size.

FLOWER: See Plate CCCXXXVI (1½ times natural size).

NOTE: A short columnar species rather larger growing than *I. bicolor*, such that the stem diameter can be as much as 5 in (12.5 cm). The rib formation is fairly straight, ranging from 15 to 23, with large oval areoles, bearing up to 12 or more fine radial spines, and up to 8 stouter centrals, the longest often exceeding ½ in (1.25 cm).

Cultural requirements as for *I. bicolor*.

Islaya solitaria *Ritt.*
(Peru)

COLOUR: Grey-green body, with creamy-white wool in the centre and on the newer areoles and pinkish-brown spines with black tips.

SIZE: Shown at just above natural size.

FLOWER: See Plate CCCXXXVII (natural size).

NOTE: Although, as with the previous species, plants are normally solitary, occasionally double-headed specimens are sometimes raised from seed, as can happen with many other cacti.

The ribs are fairly straight, up to 20 in number, bearing woolly areoles which are considerably raised, giving an almost tubercled appearance to this species. There are up to 10 radial spines and more often than not only 1 central, sometimes up to 4.

This species is by far the most free flowering species of the four we have included in this volume, but this needs the most care against rotting, such that we feel that clay pots are a must in any climate comparable to that of Britain.

Lophophora diffusa *Croiz.*
(Mexico)

COLOUR: Chalky-green to pale bluish-green body with white woolly tufts.

SIZE: Shown at about natural size.

FLOWER: Pale pink and sometimes almost a pale magenta.

NOTE: This particular species, which is also listed as *L. echinata var. diffusa Croiz.*, is quite distinct when compared with the photograph of *L. williamsii* in Volume I (page 111), which in itself is a very variable species.

This species develops large single heads and only clusters to a limited degree when compared with the illustration of *L. williamsii* overleaf and just visible at the bottom of the picture. The flowers of *L. diffusa* are at least twice the size of those of any form of *L. williamsii*.

This species is much slower growing than most forms of *L. williamsii* and, although requiring the same sandy humus soil mixture, should be watered rather carefully at all times. In winter, a minimum temperature of 40°F (5°C) is sufficient, provided it is kept dry.

Lophophora williamsii fa. cristata *Hort.*
(Mexico)

COLOUR: Grey-green to bluish-green body with small tufts of white wool.

SIZE: Shown about one-quarter natural size.

FLOWER: Small pink flowers, sometimes off-white to yellowish, with sensitive filaments, as with species of Opuntia and Wigginsia (Malacocarpus).

NOTE: In Volume I (page 111) we illustrated one of the many forms of the normal species, whereas here you can see one of our cristate specimens growing naturally in one of our raised beds.

No matter whether it is cristate or not, this is a quite slow growing species, has quite long tuberous roots and needs a sandy humus soil mixture. In Volume I, it was stated that great care should be taken over the amount of water to be given. Yet we have found in the last twenty-two years that provided the weather is warm and the soil reasonably drained, rather more water can be given. In winter, it should be kept dry, when a minimum of 40°F (5°C) is sufficient.

This particular cristate grows very well on its own roots, so that grafting is not necessary.

Notocactus crassigibbus   *Ritt.*
(Brazil)

COLOUR: Dark green body often tinged with purple, white woolly areoles and pale brown spines when new, soon changing to off-white or grey.

SIZE: Shown at about two thirds natural size.

FLOWER: See Plate CCCXXXIX (two-thirds natural size).

NOTE: This distinctive species was first described in 1970. It usually remains solitary, as with the majority of *Notocacti*. It has very prominent chins above the areole, whilst in some cases the spines can be longer than illustrated above, and are also much more twisted. Sometimes there can be 3 or 4 more spines per areole.

It is of easy culture and although not quick growing, it does well in a humus and gritty sand mixture, with plenty of water during the spring to autumn period when the weather is warm. It grows best under lightly shaded glass; if not it can become too mottled with purple and growth is severely restricted.

In winter, provided it is kept dry, a minimum of 45°F (8°C) is quite sufficient.

Notocactus rutilans *Dan & Krainz*
(Uruguay)

COLOUR: Dark green to brownish-green body, with white wool nearer the centre, and reddish-brown spines.

SIZE: Shown at slightly above natural size.

FLOWER: See Plate CCCXXXVIII (two-thirds natural size).

NOTE: There are two forms of this species, one which rarely exceeds 2 in (5 cm) in height and another which is slimmer and grows to at least twice that height.

The rib count varies from 20 to 24, straight or slightly spiralled, with up to 16 radial spines and 2 slightly longer centrals, which can be as much as $\frac{1}{4}$ in (6mm).

It is a very easy growing species, requiring a soil of about equal parts by volume of gritty sand and humus, and plenty of water during hot weather, when it should always be grown under lightly shaded glass. In winter, if left dry, it is quite safe down to 40°F (5°C).

Oroya peruviana *B. & R.*

(Central Peru)

COLOUR: Fresh green body with white areoles and golden-yellow to brown spines.

SIZE: Shown at natural size in Plate CCCXL.

FLOWER: Plate CCCXL.

NOTE: This is in fact the original species for which this genus was erected by Britton and Rose in 1920, for a plant previously described by Schumann in 1903 as *Echinocactus peruvianus.*

Unlike the previous two species, this one is of a more flattened globular habit up to 6 in (15 cm) or so in diameter, and having about 21 ribs. The areoles are quite large and elongated, bearing up to 20 spines, of which up to 5 can be centrals. The average spine length is 1 in (2.5 cm) or less.

Cultivation requirements as for *O. borchersii* var. *fuscata.*

Oroya borchersii var. fuscata *Rauh & Bckbg.*

(N. Peru)

COLOUR: Fresh green body with golden-yellow to golden-brown spines, but distinctly ginger-brown colour towards the centre of the plant.

SIZE: Shown overleaf at about two-thirds natural size.

FLOWER: Similar to that of *O. peruviana* ¾ in (2 cm) high and half that in diameter, golden-yellow.

NOTE: A solitary globular plant, becoming slightly columnar in age, when it can reach 12 in (30 cm) in height and nearly 8 in (20 cm) in diameter. On mature plants the rib count can be around 26–28, with somewhat elongated areoles, although this feature is far more pronounced on some of the other species.From the pale brown areole some 20–30 fine spines appear, of which up to 3 can be termed centrals, the longest no more than ¾ in (2 cm), most of them much less.

This genus has to be raised from seed; not a quick process with most species, and few of them are likely to flower under ten years of age. They enjoy a soil of about equal parts by volume of gritty sand and humus, with average water from spring to autumn. During very hot weather plenty of water can be given with complete safety, when we have found that they enjoy top-shelf treatment in full sun. However, as a reminder, such advice only applies to plants over three or four years of age. In winter, if left dry, a minimum temperature of 40F (5°C) is sufficient.

Oroya borchersii var. fuscata *Rauh & Bckbg.*

FOOTNOTE: Oroyas are basically high altitude plants from the Andes, the generic name being derived from the place by the name of Oroya in central Peru, where *O. peruviana* was originally found, growing in association with *Opuntia (Tephrocactus) floccosa*. In habitat these Oroyas are scarcely visible above the surrounding ground. Most species can safely withstand temperatures below freezing, as they do in habitat and can be snow covered at times. However, in cultivation where the atmospheric humidity is high in winter, it is safer to keep them at a minimum temperature which is above freezing, otherwise plants can become somewhat scarred.

Oroya laxiareolata   *Rauh & Bckbg.*
(Central Peru)

COLOUR: Green body with white areoles, whilst the spines range from golden-yellow to whitish, many of them somewhat brown towards the bases.

SIZE: Shown at slightly above natural size.

FLOWER: Similar to that of *O. peruviana* in size and form, dark carmine but golden coloured towards the base.

NOTE: Solitary species of similar form to the previous one, but rarely exceeding 6 in (15 cm) in height, with from 20 to 30 ribs. Areoles very elongated, as can be seen in the illustration, bearing up to 24 fairly stout curved spines, centrals rarely present. These range up to 1 in (2.5 cm) in length as a general rule, but a few spines can be even longer.

Cultural requirements as for *O. borchersii* var. *fuscata.*

1303

Thelocactus bicolor *B. & R.*
(S.E. Texas and Mexico)

COLOUR: Green to purplish-green body, with off-white, cream to reddish splines.

SIZE: Shown at just over half natural size.

FLOWER: See Plate CCCXLI (half natural size).

NOTE: This is a very well known species, very variable and sometimes seen wrongly named in collections. It is usually solitary, but occasionally clusters occur with the stem up to 8 in (20 cm) or more in height with straight or slightly spiralled ribs, which can range in number from 8 to 13. The spine count varies considerably with up to a possible 18 radials and 4 centrals, often only 1, the longest being up to $1\frac{1}{2}$ in (3.75 cm).

It is of easy culture, very free flowering during the summer months, growing well in a soil of about equal parts humus and gritty sand with average watering, and can be grown in full sun. In winter, it should be left dry, when a minimum temperature of 40°F (5°C) is usually sufficient unless the atmospheric humidity is very high.

Thelocactus flavidispinus   *Bckbg.*
(Nr. Marathon, Texas)

COLOUR: Pale green body with yellow spines, some of them being partly red and yellow; later becoming cream or grey with age.

SIZE: Shown at about one and a quarter times natural size.

FLOWER: Up to 4 in (10 cm) in diameter, funnel-shaped, light rose colour, filaments yellow (basal part of the stamens), petals rather pointed usually.

NOTE: Low-growing to short columnar habit, rarely exceeding 4 in (10 cm) in height, usually solitary with about 13 ribs. There can be up to 20 flat, radial spines, flattened against the plant, whilst in maturity up to 6 centrals will appear.

It is an easy growing species, although somewhat slower growing than *T. bicolor*, but requiring exactly the same cultural treatment.

This is not a well known species in cultivation, but if you compare this with *T. bicolor* it is quite distinctive. Despite this, there is considerable argument as to whether this should only be given varietal status under *T. bicolor*, and no doubt the differences of opinion will continue.

Thelocactus hexaedrophorus *B. & R.*
(Central Mexico)

COLOUR: Bluish-green to chalky-green body with dark brown spines when new, these changing often to pinkish-grey with age.

SIZE: Shown at about two-thirds natural size.

FLOWER: See Plate CCCXLII (three-quarters natural size). However, some forms of this variable species can have slightly pink outer petals.

NOTE: A very unusual, solitary, globular species, often with a spiral rib formation, although with younger plants (as in the colour plate) it has a more tubercled appearance.

The spine count can vary considerably, with up to 9 radial spines and usually 1 central, although this can be missing. When it is present annular rings are usually visible.

It is a relatively slow growing species and one with a fairly long tap-root, in most cases requiring a gritty sand and humus soil mixture, average water and grown on a top shelf once past the seedling stage. Then it should be developing the mature blue-green to chalky-green colour; otherwise treat as for *T. bicolor.*

Thelocactus conothele var. aurantiacus *Gl. & Fstr.*

(Mexico)

COLOUR: Blue-green body with white wool in the centre, white radial spines and golden-brown centrals, which pale with age.

SIZE: Shown at 1¼ times natural size in Plate CCCXLIII.

FLOWER: See Plate CCCXLIII.

NOTE: This is a solitary globular species, of quite easy culture even though it is not a fast grower. A soil of about equal parts gritty sand and humus suits it well, with average watering for most of the warmer months of the year. Because of its dense spination, full sun conditions suit adult plants very well, when they can be expected to flower regularly each year.

In winter it should be kept quite dry, when a minimum of 40°F (5°C) is quite suitable even in a climate such as ours, where the winter atmospheric humidity can be quite high at times.

This is a recently named species, just six years ago, and its unusual flower colour amongst Mexican cacti makes it very distinctive.

Thelocactus nidulans *B. & R.*

(Mexico)

COLOUR: Bluish-green to a chalky-grey coloured body, with brown to horny-yellow spines, which as they get older change to grey.

SIZE: Shown at half natural size in Plate CCCXLIV.

FLOWER: See Plate CCCXLIV.

NOTE: A relatively large growing solitary globular species, and one which always attracts attention because of the way in which the older spines tend to splinter and become soft and fibrous.

As with *T. hexaedrophorus*, much the same cultural treatment is required, although it is a much freer flowering species. In fact, our specimens usually flower singly, but producing half a dozen or more over a period of four to six weeks.

There is still considerable confusion regarding two other species, *T. rinconensis* B. & R. and *T. lophothele* B. & R., to which *T. nidulans* is related. Admittedly *T. lophothele* has real yellow flowers, whereas *T. nidulans* and *T. rinconensis* have yellowish-white to white flowers and around 13 ribs compared with about 20 for *T. nidulans*. We have been fortunate enough to study both species in habitat and have noted a certain amount of intergrading between the two.

Uebelmannia flavispina *Buin. & Bred.*
(Brazil)

COLOUR: Dark green body, masses of creamy-white wool in the centre and in the areoles away from the centre. The spines when new are black, changing to grey with age but still with black tips.

SIZE: Shown at just above natural size.

FLOWER: Small, a little over $\frac{1}{2}$ in (1.25 cm), lemon coloured.

NOTE: This species is usually solitary but rarely exceeds 8 in (20 cm) in diameter. It has between 26 and 28 straight ribs, areoles set fairly close together each bearing 5–8 straight spines not much more than $\frac{1}{4}$ in (6 mm) in length.

Knowing that it comes from a relatively heavy summer rainfall area with rather less in winter and where the temperature never falls below 60°F (16°C), its requirements are much the same as for *Discocacti* and *Melocacti* as it grows in a very well drained sandy soil.

We have been using very successfully a rather sandy humus soil mixture, growing them in clay pan-pots on a top shelf under lightly shaded glass with somewhat less than average water. In our exceptionally long and hot summer of 1976 they had extra water, and growth results were very good. In winter, we keep them dry, and have not allowed them to endure temperatures below 55°F (13°C), which is slightly lower than that encountered in the 'wild', where up to 1 in (2.5 cm) of rain can occur during each winter month.

Uebelmannia meninensis *Buin.*
(Brazil)

COLOUR: Grey-green body with creamy-white wool in the centre only, spines grey with darker tips.

SIZE: Shown at just under natural size.

FLOWER: Small, similar to that of the previous species, yellow coloured.

NOTE: This is again solitary, of similar size to that of *U. flavispina*, with 24–26 ribs. However, the formation of the plant is such that it almost has a tubercled appearance, as you can see in the illustration above. The spines are usually slightly curved, varying from 2 (as above) to 3 or 4 per areole, ranging from $\frac{1}{4}$ to $\frac{3}{4}$ in (6 to 20 mm) in length.

Cultural requirements are the same as those given for *U. flavispina*, although the growth rate of this species is slightly better.

Uebelmannia pectinifera var. pseudopectinifera
Buin. & Bred.
(Brazil)

COLOUR: Grey-green body, creamy wool in the middle, this changing to grey with age, spines grey with black tips.

SIZE: Shown at about natural size.

FLOWER: Small like those of the previous two species, greenish-yellow.

NOTE: Solitary species, globular when young, becoming somewhat columnar in age up to 10 in (25 cm) or so in height. Body surface of this species and the variety is quite rough, in contrast to that of *U. meninensis*. It has around 14–16 straight ribs, areoles set very close together, with up to 6 spines per areole, the longest up to 1 in (2.5 cm) in length.

Although this plant illustrated is relatively young, it is flowering size. Cultivation requirements as for *U. flavispina*.

MELOCACTUS GROUP

Although one species, *M. violaceus*, was illustrated in Volume III, it is only in the last ten years or so, since Volume IV was published, that a considerable variety of these plants have been available to the amateur either as young plants or, many more, in seed form. The same also applies to *Buiningia*, a relatively new genus which we are introducing for the first time along with *Discocactus*. These are also becoming available in seed form, and with the very fine results we have had grafting young ones in order to 'speed them on their way', even plants are becoming available to the collector. The *Buiningias* are fascinating plants, because of their unusual opening and closing times for their nocturnal flowers and having these lateral cephaliums. Their culture is the same as for *Melocacti* and *Discocacti* in respect of shallow clay pans, soil and temperature requirements.

In this volume we are including a further ten species of *Melocacti* as well as including four species of *Discocacti*, another genus which can only flower after the formation of a terminal cephalium. Some detailed colour illustrations are to be found in this volume on pages 1391–1392, showing just the cephaliums and flowers of *M. broadwayi*, *M. intortus*, *M. levitestatus*, *M. matanzanus*, *M. melocactoides* and *M. macracanthus*. The latter species appears in colour depicting the fruits which are fairly typical of many of the other species, although with some species they are much smaller.

Melocacti and *Discocacti*, if grown from seed and given the correct conditions, are not unduly difficult to grow, but beware of large plants complete with cephaliums as their mortality rate when moved at that age can be quite high, unless the root system is virtually intact.

A sandy humus soil mixture is ideal for these plants. Wide shallow clay pans are the best containers with top-shelf treatment under lightly shaded glass and somewhat less than average water during the spring to autumn growing period. Additional water can be given during exceptionally hot weather only, whilst in winter an absolute minimum of 50°F (10°C) is needed, when they should be kept quite dry. A little higher temperature is safer in a damp winter climate such as that of Britain. If they can stand on gravel which contains soil-heating cables for the winter, such conditions would be ideal for the safe-keeping of these most unusual but desirable plants, which once they have produced their cephaliums were nicknamed 'Turk's Cap' many years ago.

HALF-TONE PLATE

Illustrated in Volume III

Melocactus violaceus   661

Buiningia brevicylindricus   *Buin.*
(Brazil)

COLOUR: Fresh green body with creamy-white wool in the areoles and in the cephalium, and golden-yellow spines which change to grey with age.

SIZE: Shown at about half natural size.

FLOWER: See Plate CCCXLV (two-thirds natural size).

NOTE: This plant usually remains solitary when on its own roots, but will often cluster when grafted. The rib count varies from about 11 to 14, whilst the longest spines can be up to 4 in (10 cm) long. As you can see by the numerous flower remains, this species is very free flowering once maturity has been reached and the lateral cephalium has formed. In contrast *Discocacti* and *Melocacti* have terminal ones, but equally free flowering particularly, like most *Melocacti*.

In contrast to *Melocacti*, which are day flowering, this genus is nocturnal as are *Discocacti*, often opening during the night and remaining open usually until at least mid-morning the following day.

For cultural requirements, see page 1311.

Buiningia purpureus   *Buin. & Bred.*
(Brazil)

COLOUR: Dark green body with white wool in the new areoles and in the cephalium, whilst the spines are reddish-brown, but paling with age.

SIZE: Shown at about one-third natural size.

FLOWER: See Plate CCCXLVI (two-thirds natural size).

NOTE: This is somewhat taller growing than the previous species, being about 10 in (25 cm) high, but also solitary as a general rule. The rib count is usually around 14, whilst the longest spines can be up to 3 in (7.5 cm) long.

This species is also nocturnal, but it is very unusual for a night flowering plant to have such a deep magenta flower, opening during the night and usually closing by the following midday.

Although relatively slow growing, as with the previous species, it requires the same treatment as detailed on page 1311.

Discocactus albispinus *Buin. & Bred.*
(Brazil)

COLOUR: Green to pale green body with white to creamy-white spines, tending to become grey towards the tips with age.

SIZE: Shown at about two-thirds natural size.

FLOWER: Funnel-shaped, white and just over 1½ in (4 cm) in diameter.

NOTE: A very attractive species only described in 1974, usually solitary and rarely exceeding 5 in (12.5 cm) in diameter, with 12 or 13 spirally arranged ribs. There are about 12 or 13 spines per areole, including 1 or 2 centrals, the longest of which is about 3 in (7.5 cm) in length. Spines in cephaliums same colour but very fine and flexible.

For cultural requirements, see page 1311.

Discocactus boliviensis   *Bckbg.*
(Bolivia)

COLOUR: Pale green body often somewhat tinged with pink, a little white wool in the centre and off-white spines with brown tips when new. Older spines change to a dark grey-brown colour.

SIZE: Shown at about three-quarters natural size.

FLOWER: About 2 in (5 cm) in diameter, white.

NOTE: This is another flattened globular species which rarely exceeds 6 in (15 cm) in diameter. It has 12–13 ribs and 5 or 6 spines per areole, the longest only a little over 1 in (2.5 cm) in length. The plant illustrated is not of flowering size and so does not possess a cephalium. This when present on mature plants will be just 1½ in (nearly 4 cm) in diameter and made of fine spines like other species of *Discocacti* and *Melocacti*, from which the small funnel-shaped flowers appear.

For cultural requirements, see page 1311.

Discocactus hartmannii *B. & R.*

(Paraguay)

COLOUR: Olive-green body sometimes tinged with pinkish-brown, some white wool in the centre, whilst the stiff spines are golden-brown when new, but pale with age, leaving them only with darker tips.

SIZE: Shown at about natural size.

FLOWER: Similar to the previously described species, white.

NOTE: Solitary, flattened globular habit, can sometimes exceed 6 in (15 cm) in diameter in maturity, in contrast to the juvenile specimen illustrated, which is only about half that size.

It usually has 12–16 ribs, except on young specimens when only half that number may be present. The areoles are set quite closely together, bearing up to 13 spines, of which 1 is a central, the longest usually less than ½ in (12.5 mm).

Cephalium, when present, is very similar to that of the previous species. For cultural requirements, see page 1311.

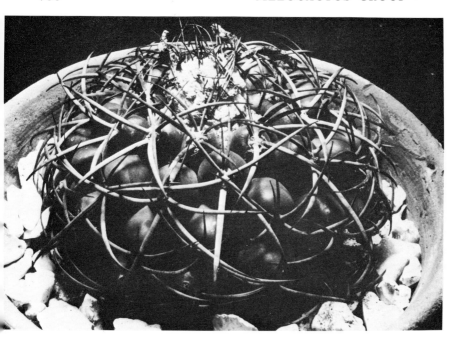

Discocactus heptacanthus *B. & R.*
(Brazil)

COLOUR: Dark shiny green body, with a little white wool on aeroles just away from the woolly centre of the plant, whilst the somewhat flattened spines are dark brown when new, changing to grey with age but still with darker tips.

SIZE: Shown at about natural size.

FLOWER: Similar to that of *D. boliviensis*, but smaller.

NOTE: Another flattened globular species, usually solitary and one which can occasionally exceed 6 in (15 cm) in diameter, and yet little more than 2 in (5 cm) in height. It has 10 or 11 rounded ribs, with the areoles, which are set in a slight spiral, well apart, giving the plant a somewhat tubercled rather than ribbed appearance.

The spines are all radials, usually 7; the longest ones can be well over 1 in (2.5 cm) in length and are always much more flattened than the short ones.

Growth of all *Discocacti* is relatively slow, and this one is no exception and should be given exactly the same treatment detailed on page 1311.

Melocactus bahiensis *Werd.*
(Brazil)

COLOUR: Dark green body with white areoles and off-white spines, except in the centre where the new ones are dark brown to black.

SIZE: Shown at about half natural size.

FLOWER: Small rose coloured flowers that last but a few hours, appearing from the cephalium, which consists of short dark brown fine spines just showing from a mass of white or off-white wool. It is very similar in appearance to that of *M. macracanthus*.

NOTE: A solitary species up to 6 in (15 cm) or more in diameter and up to 4 in (10 cm) in height. It has 10–12 straight ribs with up to 14 spines per areole, of which 2–4 are centrals, the longest a little under $1\frac{1}{2}$ in (3.75 cm).

For cultural requirements, see page 1311.

Melocactus broadwayi   *Bckbg.*
(Islands of Tobago and Grenada)

COLOUR: Pale green body with some white wool in the centre, even before the cephalium appears, and brown spines.

SIZE: Shown at about half natural size.

FLOWER: See Plate CCCXLIX (natural size).

NOTE: This is also a solitary species, as can be seen above, but one which grows more columnar in habit, even before the cephalium appears, up to 8 in (20 cm) in height. Unlike some of the species illustrated in this book, the cephalium is not huge, rarely exceeding $1\frac{1}{2}$ in (3.75 cm) in height.

It has 14–16 straight ribs, but as can be seen above, there is a chin-like protrusion between each areole. There can be up to 12 or more spines, usually only 1 central but sometimes more, the longest not more than $\frac{1}{2}$ in (1.25 cm).

For cultural requirements, see page 1311.

Melocactus communis *Lk. & O.*
(Jamaica)

COLOUR: Pale green body with yellowish spines.

SIZE: Shown at about one-third natural size.

FLOWER: Flower somewhat larger than usual, up to $\frac{1}{2}$ in (1.25 cm) or more in diameter.

NOTE: A fiercely spined species, globular in habit, with a diameter of up to 12 in (30 cm), excluding the cephalium, which can more than double its height on an old specimen.

Rib count varies considerably from 10 to 14, sometimes even more, straight, with up to 12 curved spines per areole, of which 3 can be counted as centrals, the longest sometimes exceeding 1 in (2.5 cm).

The cephalium can be quite columnar in age, consisting of whitish wool and masses of fine purplish-brown spines. As with *M. intortus* and *M. macracanthus* plants have to be quite large before the cephalium starts to appear; the plant illustrated is twenty years old and still no sign of one appearing.

For cultural requirements, see page 1311.

Melocactus ernestii   *Vpl.*
(Brazil)

COLOUR: Green body and a little white wool on the areoles nearer the centre of a juvenile plant, whilst the spines are brown, becoming black with age on old mature specimens.

SIZE: Shown at about natural size.

FLOWER: Small, magenta-rose colour, similar in form to that of most other species of *Melocacti* in the colour plates showing the flower and cephalium detail.

NOTE: This is also solitary, globular to short columnar habit eventually with 10–12 straight ribs and up to 10 spines per areole. There is usually only 1 central spine, but the interesting point to notice with this species is that the longest one is not the central but the bottom most radial, which can sometimes be as much as 3 in (7.5 cm) long on an old specimen.

The cephalium on this species can be quite tall, 5–6 in (12.5–15 cm), similar in appearance to that of *M. intortus* shown on page 1322.

For cultural requirements, see page 1311.

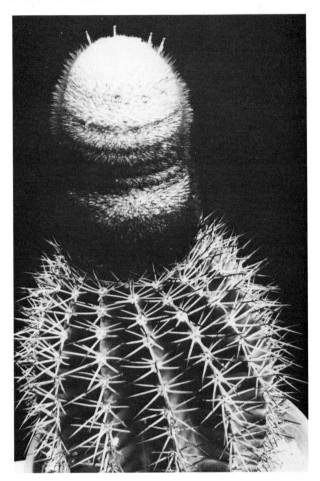

Melocactus intortus *Urb.*
(West Indies)

COLOUR: Green body with yellowish-brown to dark brown spines.

SIZE: Shown at about quarter natural size.

FLOWER: See Plate CCCXLVII (half natural size).

NOTE: This species develops a tall cephalium that can be as much as 3 ft (1 m) in length, which resulted in that nickname of Turk's Cap.

It is a globular to cylindrical species, usually solitary although branched specimens have been found up to 12–18 in (30–50 cm) in height without including the height of the cylindrical cephalium. The rib count varies considerably, anything from 14 to 20, usually straight with up to 15 stout spines per areole, the longest of which can vary from 2 to 3 in (5 to 7.5 cm).

For cultural requirements, see page 1311.

Melocactus levitestatus   *Buin. & Bred.*
(Brazil)

COLOUR: Pale green to bluish-green body with pinkish-grey spines.

SIZE: Shown at about one-quarter natural size.

FLOWER: See Plate CCCXLVIII (two-thirds natural size).

NOTE: This is quite a recent discovery, having been first described in 1973. It is a most attractive species, solitary but very columnar in habit, up to 12 in (30 cm) or more in height and around 8 in (20 cm) in diameter. There are 14–15 ribs, which are usually somewhat spiralled, bearing up to 12 spines including the 2 centrals. These are all quite stiff and the radials tend to twist in various directions to a limited degree.

The cephalium rarely exceeds 2 in (5 cm) in height but can reach up to $3\frac{1}{2}$ in (over 8 cm) in diameter, and consists of white wool and fine reddish spines. The flowers of most *Melocacti* are in shades of pink or even magenta; this one is rather unusual in having real red flowers.

For cultural requirements, see page 1311.

Melocactus macracanthus *Link & Otto*
(Dutch West Indies)

COLOUR: Dark green body with numerous stiff spines that can range from creamy-brown to reddish-brown to nearly black. In fact, they are very variable in colour, sometimes even on the same plant, and this also applies to their stoutness. This is demonstrated by the two illustrations opposite of juvenile (non-flowering size) plants.

SIZE: Illustration *above* shown at one-fifth natural size. Illustrations *opposite* shown at two-thirds natural size.

FLOWER: Small pinkish-magenta, appearing singly or a few together in rings from the cephalium, sometimes alongside fully ripened fruits. Colour Plate CCCL shows cephalium with fruits (at half natural size).

NOTE: This species has been known for a very long time and because of its variability of form has the dubious distinction of possessing more synonyms than any other cactus known!

It is a solitary globular species up to 12 in (30 cm) in diameter with 11–15 straight ribs, bearing up to 15–20 spines per areole, one of which is usually the central. All spines are stout, the longest one being the central which is usually present, and this can be up to 3 in (7.5 cm) long.

For cultural requirements, see page 1311.

Melocactus macracanthus *Link & Otto*
Two differing specimens.

Melocactus matanzanus *Leon*
(Cuba)

COLOUR: Green body with brown spines changing to grey, whilst cephalium has masses of fine bright red spines.

SIZE: Shown at just above natural size.

FLOWER: See Plate CCCLI (half natural size).

NOTE: This is the real miniature of this genus, usually solitary and less than 4 in (10 cm) in diameter and slightly less than that in height. The cephalium can eventually reach $2\frac{1}{2}$ in (6.25 cm) in diameter and not much more than $1\frac{1}{2}$ in (3.75 cm) in height.

There are usually no more than 8 or 9 straight ribs, a slight chin protuberance between the areole positions, from which 7 or 8 radial spines and 1 erect central appear, all of similar length, around $\frac{1}{3}$ in (about 8 mm).

It is a relatively easy growing species, provided the usual temperature requirements are kept to in winter, easily raised from seed and under the right conditions a cephalium can start to form in five to seven years even with our short growing season. We know of people who have reached this stage in three years, but that is in a much more tropical climate with a long growing season.

For cultural requirements, see page 1311.

Melocactus maxonii   *Gurke*
(Guatemala)

COLOUR: Dark green body with brown spines that later change to grey, but often still leaving them with a dark tip.

SIZE: Shown at about natural size.

FLOWER: Slightly larger than those of some of the species illustrated in colour; rose-red appearing from amidst the snowy-white cephalium.

NOTE: This is not a large growing species, rarely exceeding 6 in (15 cm) in height, but always slightly columnar in habit. The rib count can vary from 11 to 15, narrow and straight with quite large circular areoles. There are 8–10 radial spines, all stout and flattened against the plant, whilst the central one stands straight out and can occasionally exceed 1 in (2.5 cm) in length.

For cultural requirements, see page 1311.

Melocactus melocactoides *DC.*
(Brazil)

COLOUR: Dark green body with grey spines that have dark tips.

SIZE: Shown at about natural size.

FLOWER: See Plate CCCLII (two-thirds natural size).

NOTE: This is also a small growing solitary species like *M. matanzanus*, but can reach up to 6 in (15 cm) in diameter and just over 3 in (7.5 cm) in height, excluding the height of the cephalium. There are usually about 10 straight ribs, between 5 and 8 radial spines only per areole, these about 1 in (2.5 cm) long.

It is a very attractive species, very free flowering from quite early in the spring to late autumn but somewhat slower growing than *M. matanzanus* and requires much the same cultural treatment as the other species as detailed on page 1311.

MAMMILLARIA GROUP

Just one new genus, *Solisia*, is being included this time in addition to a further 30 species which belong in this group within the following genera—*Coryphantha, Escobaria, Mammillaria* and *Pelecyphora*.

The genus *Solisia* is a monotypic one—that is, containing but one species. It is, in fact, a much sought after plant because of its miniature habit and the fact that it is so densely covered with white pectinate spines such that the body of the plant cannot be seen. It has been transferred by some authorities to the genus *Mammillaria* as *M. pectinifera*.

In addition to including some further species of *Coryphantha, Escobaria* and *Pelecyphora*, we have made a special point of including a number of Mammillarias which in some cases had not even been described when Volume IV was published, let alone been in general cultivation. Yet, in that short space of time, such beautiful large flowered miniatures as *M. goldii, M. saboae* and *M. theresae* are almost commonplace in collections today. In addition to these, we have also included a variety of the larger flowered, hooked spined species, some of which come from Baja California in Mexico, which were also rarities only twelve years ago in collections. It is for this reason that 14 species are included in the colour section to show the detail and full beauty of these fine plants.

M. guelzowiana was known as *Krainzia guelzowiana* Bckbg., a genus erected by Backeberg in honour of Dr H. Krainz who was Curator of the 'Succulent Collection' in Zurich, Switzerland. His reason for separating 'guelzowiana' from the genus *Mammillaria* was based on the unusual flower characteristics and certain seed details. Most authorities today do not consider that the genus name *Krainzia* is a valid one. Another species also included here is *M. longiflora*, which was also included by Backeberg in the genus *Krainzia*.

COLOUR PLATES
Illustrated in Volume III

COLOUR PLATES
Illustrated in Volume IV

Coryphantha poselgeriana *B. & R.*
(Mexico)

COLOUR: Grey-green to pale chalky-blue body, some off-white wool between the tubercles on the upper half of the plant. Greyish spines, somewhat bulbous at their bases, reddish-brown to black when new.

SIZE: Shown at about half natural size.

FLOWER: See Plate CCCLIII (two-thirds natural size).

NOTE: A slow growing globular species up to 8 in (20 cm) or so in height and diameter, with prominent angular tubercles as can be seen in the illustration above. The spines are also thick and stiff, compared with the other species in this genus included in this volume.

A sandy humus mixture is required, less than average water at all times from spring to autumn, doing best on a top shelf, even if it is in full sun.

In winter, if dry, a minimum of 40°F (5°C) is sufficient, but higher if cold and damp. It is a very fine species, the plant being very distinctive whilst the flowers are most unusual and can exceed $2\frac{1}{2}$ in (6.25 cm) in diameter.

Coryphantha ramillosa *Cutak*
(Texas)

COLOUR: Rather soft dark green body, areoles whitish bearing white radial spines and slender brown centrals, these somewhat grey towards their bases.

SIZE: Shown at about two-thirds natural size.

FLOWER: 2 in (5 cm) in diameter, pale pink to rose-purple.

NOTE: It is usually solitary and can reach nearly 8 in (20 cm) in diameter, some forms being more densely spined than the specimen illustrated above. The spines are very pliable, particularly the centrals.

A soil of about equal parts gritty sand and humus is ideal, average water from spring to autumn, extra in very hot weather when best results are obtained under lightly shaded glass. Older plants which have been flowering for a year or so can safely cope with full sun conditions without burning, despite the fact that this is quite a soft bodied species.

In winter, if kept dry, it is quite safe down to only a degree or so above freezing point, even in a damp winter climate.

Coryphantha sulcata *B. & R.*
(Texas)

COLOUR: Fresh green body with off-white to cream radial and central spines.

SIZE: Shown at about natural size.

FLOWER: See Plate CCCLIV (two-thirds natural size).

NOTE: This is a very easy-growing and free flowering clustering species of a low growing habit. The diameter of fully grown heads can reach up to 4 in (10 cm) or so in diameter, but can be much less than this and still flower well. It forms into quite large flattish mounds.

It grows well in a soil which contains at least 50% of humus, likes plenty of water throughout the growing season under lightly shaded glass. Unlike some of the other softer and thinner skinned *Coryphantha*, this one seems less prone to attack by 'red-spider'.

In winter, provided it is quite dry, it can safely withstand temperatures down to near or even a little below freezing point.

Escobaria aguirreana comb. nov.
(Mexico)

COLOUR: Dark green body, with either whitish radial spines and darker tips or even orange to plum coloured, whilst the centrals vary from off-white near the bases to brownish-black towards the tips.

SIZE: Shown at nearly twice natural size.

FLOWER: Just over $\frac{1}{2}$ in (1.25 cm) long, yellowish to reddish-yellow and due to the dense spination unable to open very much.

NOTE: Unlike *E. roseana* overleaf, this species is usually solitary, rarely exceeding 2 in (5 cm) in height and 3 in (7.5 cm) in diameter. It is also fairly slow growing, requiring a sandy humus soil mixture, slightly less than average water from spring to autumn, when all but seedling plants can grow in full sun conditions. In winter it should be left dry, with a minimum of 40°F (5°C).

It was first discovered in 1970 and named *Gymnocactus aguirreanus* Gl. & Fstr., in honour of Ing. Gustavo Aguirre. However, we usually prefer to follow the Britton & Rose classification, hence its inclusion amongst the Escobarias. This being one of the newer species, it is also illustrated in colour (Plate CCCLVII) showing a much darker spined form in bloom at $1\frac{1}{4}$ times natural size.

Escobaria roseana *Bkbg.*
(Mexico)

COLOUR : Bright green body partially obscured by numerous fine golden-yellow spines

SIZE : Shown at just under natural size.

FLOWER : See Plate CCCLVIII (natural size).

NOTE : This is a very easy growing and free flowering species, which has only been made available to the amateur in the last few years. It is low growing and can grow into large clumps of many dozens of heads.

A soil containing at least 50% of humus seems ideal, with plenty of water during the warmer months of the year, when it will grow equally well under lightly shaded glass or in full sun. It is also well suited to 'bed' rather than pot culture, when quicker growth and more flowers can be expected.

Culture as for *E. aguirreana*.

Mammillaria armillata   *K. Brand*
(Baja California)

COLOUR: Green bodied plant, somewhat obscured by the white radial spines, these appearing from white areoles along with one golden-brown hooked central spine. Occasionally, this hooked central can be missing

SIZE: Shown at just above natural size.

FLOWER: Pale pink, up to 1 in (2.5 cm) in diameter.

NOTE: This is the first of the range of hooked spined species which also have large flowers to be included in this book, from Baja California. When Volume IV was published, many of these species, although known to exist, were very poorly represented in collections, but today many amateurs possess some of these fine species.

Unlike the majority of *Mammillaria*, they require more careful cultivation and we find that a gritty sand and humus mixture is ideal, plus top-shelf culture. They need less than average water from spring to autumn unless the weather is exceptionally hot when extra can be given, beneath lightly shaded glass and preferably using a clay pot.

Although a minimum temperature in winter of 40–45°F (5–8°C) is sufficient, a higher minimum is necessary if the atmospheric humidity is high.

Mammillaria boolii   *Linds.*
(Mexico)

COLOUR: Body of the plant green, but this is to a large degree obscured by the spreading, fine white radial spines. There is only one central spine; this is hooked and yellow in colour but with more brown on the upper half.

SIZE: Shown at about one and a half times natural size.

FLOWER: See Plate CCCLIX (twice natural size).

NOTE: A small growing species up to 2 in (5 cm) in height and slightly less than that in diameter. As a general rule, it remains solitary. However, we have seen a few odd branched specimens, but this is rather unusual unless seedlings have been grafted at a young age, when this sometimes occurs. In fact, with some of the other miniature large flowered species such as *M. goldii, M. saboae* and *M. theresae* illustrated in this volume, this is the easiest way to propagate them, as they cluster very freely on a graft.

M. boolii likes a well drained soil, somewhat less than average water during the growing season (unless the weather is very hot, when extra can be given), and top-shelf treatment under lightly shaded glass. In winter, a minimum temperature of 40–45°F (5–8°C) is sufficient, when it should be left completely dry.

Mammillaria capensis *Craig*
(Baja California)

COLOUR: Dark green body, with very prominent tubercles bearing white radial spines and one central, this latter spine being reddish-brown when new, soon changing to off-white or white.

SIZE: Shown at about three-quarters natural size.

FLOWER: See Plate CCCLV (natural size).

NOTE: This is the second of a number of large flowered, hooked spined species which we are including in this volume, the majority of which come from the Baja California peninsula, the part of Mexico which is separated from the mainland of Mexico by the Gulf of California.

It is a clustering species, but stems rarely exceed 4 in (10 cm) in height. The half-tone illustration was filmed during the winter rest period and shows the plant in a much more compact form, compared with the colour plate (CCCLV), when the plant had filled out and was growing.

Mammillaria craigii   *Linds.*
(Mexico)

COLOUR: Dark green body with some white wool towards the apex, with beautiful golden-brown radial and central spines.

SIZE: Shown at about two-thirds natural size.

FLOWER: Dark pink to almost magenta.

NOTE: A very attractive solitary species, which can eventually divide dichotomously and grow into quite a large specimen. It is of easy culture, enjoying a soil of equal parts gritty sand and humus and needing a fairly ample supply of water during the spring to autumn period, provided the weather is fairly warm and it is kept under lightly shaded glass.

In winter, provided it is kept dry, a minimum temperature of 40°F (5°C) is quite sufficient; flower buds often start developing in late February before one thinks of watering. There are other cacti that do this, but it is not necessary to start watering at this time, unless you wish to keep such plants in much warmer conditions for the remainder of the winter.

Mammillaria crucigera   *Mart.*
(Mexico)

COLOUR: Pale green body with brown areoles and short white radial spines.

SIZE: Shown at just above natural size.

FLOWER: Flower small, less than ½ in (1.25 cm), deep red to purple with narrow acute petals.

NOTE: A slow growing species which clusters by dividing dichotomously (single heads into two, grow on to full size and then repeat the process).

It requires a sandy humus soil mixture with less than average water at all times—unless the weather is exceptionally hot—and grows best under lightly shaded glass.

In winter, a minimum temperature of 45°F (8°C) is to be preferred, when it should be kept quite dry. It is still an uncommon species in cultivation, but becoming better known now.

Mammillaria estebanensis *Linds.*
(Baja California)

COLOUR: Pale green body almost obscured by the mass of white radial spines, also one hooked central, off-white to pale brown at the base, but much darker brown at the tip. The central spine can sometimes be straight or absent.

SIZE: Shown at about three-quarters natural size.

FLOWER: See Plate CCCLX (two-thirds natural size).

NOTE: Although shown as a solitary plant, it does cluster and plants of up to 50 heads have been observed. This plant was first described in 1967, having been named after one of the two islands in the Gulf of California on which it was originally discovered—San Esteban Island; it also occurs on San Lorenzo Island.

It is not a fast growing species, but can be treated as for *M. armillata*.

It grows on the same island as *Echinocereus grandis*, which is also included in this volume.

Mammillaria fraileana   *B. & R.*
(Baja California)

COLOUR: Dark green body nearly obscured by the radial spines, which are off-white, sometimes tinged with pink. One of the central spines is hooked and dark brown towards the tip.

SIZE: Shown at slightly above natural size.

FLOWER: See Plate CCCLVI (1¼ times natural size).

NOTE: This is another of the larger flowered species in this genus, related to such species as *M. blossfeldiana* and *M. microcarpa var. auricarpa* described and illustrated in Volume IV of this series. It does cluster to a degree with age, exceedingly free flowering, this occurring usually some weeks after most other species within the genus have finished flowering.

As with most of the other large flowered and hooked spined species, a fairly well drained growing mixture is required and less than average water at all times. In winter, complete dryness is essential and a minimum temperature of 40–45°F (5–8°C).

Mammillaria glassii *R. A. Fstr.*
(Mexico)

COLOUR: Green body sometimes quite pale, but almost entirely obscured by the white hairs from between the tubercles and the bristle-like golden-brown spines and one hooked central.

SIZE: Shown at about one and a half times natural size.

FLOWER: Flowers very early, often in March, very pale pink

NOTE: Although it is not a particularly slow grower, it is one which must be watered with care, unless the weather is very hot, and because of this it does require a rather sandy humus soil mixture, to ensure good drainage. It grows best under lightly shaded glass, even though the body of the plant is well protected by the hair and spines.

In winter, it must be kept dry, as it is very prone to rotting off, and where atmospheric humidity is high a minimum of 45°F (8°C) is essential, or even a little higher.

It is certainly a very distinctive new species, which only bears a superficial resemblance to *M. albicoma* and *M. bocasana*, and one which can be equally easily propagated from seed or offsets.

Mammillaria goldii   *Gl. & Fstr.*
(Mexico)

COLOUR: Green body with small white areoles and very soft fine white radial spines.

SIZE: Shown at nearly twice natural size.

FLOWER: See Plate CCCLXI (three-quarters natural size).

NOTE: This is the first of three large flowered miniature *Mammillaria* which are being included in this volume; this one was named only in 1968, in honour of a very good friend of ours, Dudley Gold, who has spent over fifty years exploring in various parts of Mexico.

It is, in fact, a very easy growing miniature species, enjoying a soil of about equal part humus and sand, with plenty of water during the spring to autumn period, provided the weather is warm.

In winter, it should be kept dry, when plants will tend to pull themselves down into the soil, and a minimum temperature of 40–45°F (5–8°C) is sufficient.

Mammillaria guelzowiana *Werd.*
(Mexico)

COLOUR: Body of the plant green, almost bluish-green at times, whilst some of the older tubercles can develop a reddish tinge. The tubercles which are soft bear a little yellowish-white wool and numerous long white hair-like radial spines, plus one hooked central spine. This hooked spine rarely exceeds ½ in (1.25 cm) in length, and is reddish-brown in colour.

SIZE: Shown at slightly above natural size.

FLOWER: See Plates CCCLXIII and CCCLXIV (both natural size).

NOTE: This is a very beautiful species, like an enlarged *M. bocasana*, except that this species often remains solitary. However, the flower is exceptionally large with a 2 in (5 cm) long tube and an even wider spread.

It needs a well-drained soil, less than average water during the growing season, unless the weather is very hot, when extra can be given. It seems to grow and flower equally well under lightly shaded glass or in full sun, but top-shelf treatment is advised at all times. It is essential in winter that it is kept quite dry, when plants will shrivel a certain amount, and that drips from condensation on the glass never fall on it at that time of year. A winter minimum temperature of 45°F (8°C) is advised for this species.

Mammillaria longiflora   *B. & R.*
(Mexico)

COLOUR: Fresh green body, often somewhat paler between the bases of the tubercles, which bear a little white wool at the areole positions. White radial spines and up to 4 centrals, one of which is hooked and changing from off-white at the base to brown at the hooked tip.

SIZE: Shown at just above natural size.

FLOWER: See Plate CCCLXII (twice natural size).

NOTE: This species with its large flowers is native to much higher altitudes near Durango. It grows well in a well drained soil but even in the adult stage should be grown under lightly shaded conditions. During very hot weather, extra water can be given, whilst in winter dryness is essential, when plants will tend to shrivel and pull themselves down into the soil a little. It can be safely kept at temperatures nearer freezing point (in drier climates), unlike the Mammillarias from Baja California described in this volume. However, in a damper climate a minimum of 45°F (8°C) is safer. Backeberg also included this species in the genus *Krainzia*.

Mammillaria louisae   *Linds.*
(Baja California)

COLOUR: Pale green body with the tubercles bearing fine white radial
spines, whilst one of the centrals is hooked, brown in colour
with a darker tip.

SIZE: Shown at just one and a half times natural size.

FLOWER: See Plate CCCLXV (natural size).

NOTE: In contrast to *M. fraileana* where stems can grow to 4 in (10 cm)
or more in length, the stems of this species rarely grow to more than half that
size. Unlike the other hooked spined and large flowered Mammillarias illustrated in this volume, this one even in the adult state grows best under slightly
shaded glass at all times. A similar soil to that recommended for *M. fraileana*
is suitable, but a little more water will be required during the growing season,
particularly if the weather is very hot.

Winter requirements are the same, with a minimum of 40–45°F (5–8°C).

Mammillaria mercadensis   *Pat.*
(Mexico)

COLOUR : Green to sometimes brownish-green, if plants have been insufficiently shaded, with off-white radial spines and brown to reddish-brown centrals.

SIZE : Shown at about one and a half times natural size.

FLOWER : Off-white to pale rose, with a slightly darker median stripe on each petal.

NOTE : This species can be solitary or clustering, but it is always quite dwarf in habit and one which requires a somewhat sandy humus soil mixture with slightly less than average water during the normal growing period. It requires top-shelf treatment under partially shaded glass for best results.

In winter, however, a minimum of 45°F (8°C) is low enough in a damp climate such as ours, when it is absolutely essential that plants remain quite dry.

It is a far from common species in collections today, but a number of fine flowering plants can be seen in 'The Exotic Collection' and these can always be relied upon to flower very freely each year.

Mammillaria multidigitata *Linds.*
(Baja California)

COLOUR: Fresh green body with off-white areoles and radial spines and usually one brown straight central spine, but up to four have been known.

SIZE: Shown at about two-thirds natural size.

FLOWER: See Plate CCCLXVII.

NOTE: This species is also native to Baja California, or to be more exact of San Pedro Nolasco Island in the Gulf of California, where clumps with up to a hundred or more heads have been known, hence its specific name meaning 'many fingers'. The radial spine count varies considerably and there can be up to 4 centrals.

Unlike most of the hooked spined species from the same area, the flowers of this species are somewhat smaller, being only just over $\frac{1}{2}$ in (1.25 cm) in diameter.

It is a relatively easy growing species, although a reasonably well drained soil is still needed, and grown under lightly shaded glass. Dry conditions in winter are important when the same minimum temperature requirements also apply, as with the other species from this part of Mexico.

Mammillaria oliviae *Orcutt*

(Arizona, New Mexico, Texas and neighbouring parts of Mexico)

COLOUR: Green body completely obscured by the white spines.

SIZE: Shown at natural size in Plate CCCLXVIII.

FLOWER: See Plate CCCLXVIV.

NOTE: This species also remains solitary usually like *M. wrightii*, and can grow up to 4 in (10 cm) in height with a diameter of 2½–3 in (6.25–7.5 cm). It is very densely spined, mostly radials flattened against the plant along with longer centrals, sometimes with dark tips up to ⅓ in (8 mm) in length, usually curved, occasionally slightly hooked.

This species in nature does sometimes hybridise with *M. microcarpa* and it is possible that specimens with a few hooked spines could be hybrids with *M. microcarpa*, where a prominent hooked central is always present. This was certainly true of specimens studied by us on the Santa Cruz County/Pima County, border in Arizona.

This species, as with *M. boolii* and the many forms of *M. microcarpa*, flowers during late July and early August in Britain, whereas most of the Baja Californian Mammillarias included in this volume flower (usually sporadically) from June onwards for a minimum of two months and sometimes longer.

This species needs the same cultural treatment as *M. boolii*. It may also be seen under the name *M. grahamii var. oliviae* L. Benson.

Mammillaria pennispinosa *Krainz*
(Mexico)

COLOUR: Green body almost completely obscured by the creamy-white to pale pink and orange-pink plumose (feathery) radial spines and the brown hooked central.

SIZE: Shown at about one and a half times natural size.

FLOWER: Off-white with a rose coloured median stripe on each petal.

NOTE: This is a very beautiful little species, usually solitary, and can reach up to $1\frac{1}{2}$ in (3.75 cm) in height and diameter.

It is not a fast growing species, but can even here be flowered in its third year from seed. It does need a somewhat sandy humus soil mixture, top-shelf treatment and slightly less than average water under lightly shaded glass.

It is most attractive and flowers freely in the spring over many weeks, but because of the beautiful plumose radial spines it is always attractive. The pink to orange-pink spined form is the most common.

In winter, it must be kept dry, when it is quite safe down to 45°F (8°C), and if the atmospheric humidity is low a lower temperature is quite safe.

Mammillaria pennispinosa var. nazasensis *Gl. & Fstr.*
(Mexico)

COLOUR: Green body just visible through the white to off-white radial spines and creamy-yellow centrals.

SIZE: Shown at just above natural size.

FLOWER: Creamy-white with only a very pale median stripe on each petal.

NOTE: This variety differs from the type species described on the previous page by not having plumose radial spines, although they are slightly hirsute (hairy or pubescent), whilst the spines are uniformly pale in colour.

Its cultivation requirements are the same as those for the type species in all respects.

This is a recently described species (1975), although it was originally discovered in 1968, growing among boulders near the Rio Nazas in the state of Durango, which is about 100 miles from the nearest locality for *M. pennispinosa*.

Mammillaria saboae *Glass*
(Mexico)

COLOUR: Pale green body with small white areoles and short fine white spines.

SIZE: Shown at about one and a half times natural size.

FLOWER: See Plate CCCLXVI (natural size).

NOTE: This is the second of the three new miniature Mammillarias with large flowers, this one discovered by Mrs Kitty Sabo and her son at around 7,000 ft (2,300 m) on the eastern side of the Sierra Madre Occidental in Chihuahua.

The specimen above was photographed in the winter resting period. The fruits on this *Mammillaria* and some of the other species in this group (Section *Phellosperma* Moran) remain within the body of the plant when ripe. It is thought that as the plants move up and down in the soil, according to the season, this allows some of the seeds to be dispersed—or this may happen when a plant dies and presumably such seeds have a very long life.

The cultural requirements for this species are exactly the same as for *M. goldii* on page 1345.

Mammillaria schumannii   *Hild.*
(Baja California)

COLOUR: Grey-green body visible through the spines, the radials being white whilst one of the centrals is hooked and reddish-brown towards the tip.

SIZE: Shown at slightly above natural size.

FLOWER: See Plate CCCLXXI (1¼ times natural size).

NOTE: This is another large flowered species of similar habit to *M. fraileana* (page 1343) and requiring identical cultural treatment. It is a very free flowering plant, the flower occurring at about the same time as *M. fraileana*. This form has longer hooked spines and a more open structure. Others can be more compact, with slightly shorter tubercles and spines.

For a very long time this plant was known under the generic heading *Bartschella* B. & R., but nowadays it is generally listed as a *Mammillaria*. It was originally separated from the genus *Mammillaria* because the fruit did not become elongated and only protruded at maturity, plus a few other lesser features. Those readers possessing earlier editions of Volume I should ignore or delete the reference to *Bartschella* on page 152.

Mammillaria standleyi   *Orcutt*
(Mexico)

COLOUR: Greenish body with plenty of white wool between the tubercles, particularly towards the apex, with white radial spines and brownish centrals.

SIZE: Shown at about half natural size.

FLOWER: Magenta coloured with a darker median line on each petal.

NOTE: A variable form, some being solitary, whilst others like this one can eventually form into clumps up to 3 ft (1 m) across. The solitary ones are more common in habitat at a lower elevation in the canyons of the Sierra de Alamos in the state of Sonora. Also, they have slightly longer radial spines, more of them, such that they cross one another. In contrast, those specimens from higher up (as illustrated) are densely clustering, shorter spined, etc.

It is a very easy growing and free flowering species that enjoys a soil of about equal parts gritty sand and humus, average watering and once past the seedling stage can take full sun conditions. Its flowering qualities are not impeded if grown with other species under lightly shaded glass.

In winter, if dry, it is quite safe down to 40°F (5°C).

Mammillaria theresae *Cutak*
(Mexico)

COLOUR: Dark green body often tinged with purple, white areoles and soft white plumose radial spines.

SIZE: Shown at about 1¼ times natural size.

FLOWER: See Plate CCCLXIX (1¼ times natural size).

NOTE: An exceedingly easy growing dwarf species like *M. goldii* and *M. saboae* and which eventually forms into quite large flat growing clusters.

A soil of about equal parts of humus and gritty sand, with plenty of water in warm weather, but less during cooler conditions. It can cope with full sun conditions, but best results are obtained under lightly shaded glass.

In winter, it should be kept dry, when plants shrink a little, with a minimum temperature of 40–45°F (5–8°C).

Grafted specimens are sometimes seen of this species, which tend to be more open in appearance, whereby the areoles are further apart. It is a good way of propagating them as they will branch more freely. However, although slower, they are equally easy to grow on their own roots.

Mammillaria wrightii   *Engelm.*
(Arizona, New Mexico, Texas and neighbouring parts of Mexico)

COLOUR: Body of the plant green, brown radial spines changing to grey or even white, and usually three dark brown hooked centrals.

SIZE: Shown at about one-third above natural size.

FLOWER: See Plate CCCLXX (twice natural size).

NOTE: This is a small growing species, usually solitary, globose to short cylindrical, and has been recorded as growing up to 4 in (10 cm) in height, but is normally much less than this.

There is considerable variation of this species, whereby some authorities consider that *M. wilcoxii* Toumey and *M. viridiflora* Bdkr. are also just variations of *M. wrightii*. As with other cacti that we have studied in habitat, this one is no exception in that some forms not only have more radial spines, but are also much finer (in some cases). The flowers not only differ in colour, but some forms also open wider than the specimen in Plate CCCLXX.

This species does have some similarities to *M. grahamii* Engelm., whereas *M. oliviae*, illustrated only in colour, is very distinctive.

M. wrightii requires the same cultural treatment as *M. boolii*.

Pelecyphora pseudopectinata *Bckbg.*
(Mexico)

COLOUR: The green body is almost entirely obscured by the mass of slender white pectinate spine clusters on each tubercle.

SIZE: Shown at about twice natural size.

FLOWER: See Plate CCCLXXII (twice natural size).

NOTE: This is usually solitary, as is *P. valdeziana* (overleaf), in contrast to *P. aselliformis* which was illustrated in colour on page 404 of Volume II. Although shown only as a single head, it can grow into quite large clusters in age, as can be seen by visiting subscribers of 'The Exotic Collection' (see page 1498).

It grows well in a sandy humus soil mixture with slightly less than average water, on a top shelf and under lightly shaded glass. It often flowers in Britain in March; in fact the illustration above was photographed in mid-January and the first flower bud is already visible. Readers in the southern hemisphere would flower this plant usually around August or September. In winter, it should be kept dry and is quite safe down to 40–45°F (5–8°C) or even lower, as in its native habitat around San Luis Potosi it occasionally endures quite low temperatures down to near freezing point.

Pelecyphora valdeziana *Moeller*
(Mexico)

COLOUR: The white or off-white plumose (feathered) pectinate spines completely obscure the green body colour of this plant. In age these delicate feathery spines disappear, leaving a greyish-brown corky base, which is in fact the woody remains of the tubercles.

SIZE: Shown at about 2½ times natural size.

FLOWER: See Plate CCCLXXIII (1¼ times natural size).

NOTE: This is a slow growing miniature species, almost always solitary, but like *P. pseudopectinata* is of easy culture provided a similar well drained soil is used, and given the same treatment. Its flowering period, however, is not quite so early as *P. pseudopectinata*. It requires identical winter conditions as well.

This is the same plant as *Thelocactus valdezianus* Bdkr. and *Gymnocactus valdezianus* Bckbg., whilst more recently the name *Normanbokea* has been produced for just this one plant to cause even greater confusion. However, we feel that the reasons put forward for such a transfer are not sufficient to warrant it, at a time when there is already a proliferation of names. As with *Ariocarpus kotschoubeyanus*, there is a white flowered form of this particular *Pelecyphora*, but this again does not warrant varietal status as put forward by Pazout in 'Kaktusy' in 1960.

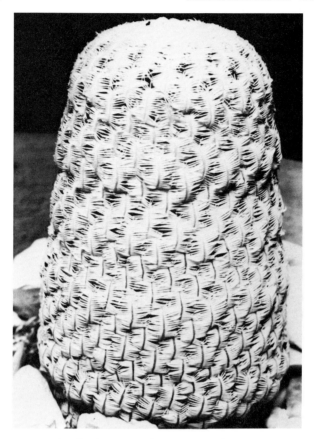

Solisia pectinata *B. & R.*
(Mexico)

COLOUR: In exactly the same way as for *P. valdeziana*, the white pectinate spines completely obscure the green body of the plant.

SIZE: Shown at over 2½ times natural size.

FLOWER: Small, pink to magenta flowers similar to those of a Mammillaria appear from the side of a plant, just below the crown.

NOTE: Another slow growing, solitary, short columnar miniature plant; the only described species within the genus and can therefore be described as a monotypic genus.

After the seedling stage, it is not unduly difficult to grow, given a sandy humus growing mixture and less than average water for much of the growing season— in other words, identical treatment to that for *Pelecyphora pseudopectinata*. Unlike the Pelecyphoras, which are in more general cultivation today, this one is still a rarity.

A winter minimum temperature of 40–45°F (5–8°C) is advised for this plant, when it should be kept dry.

EPIPHYLLUM AND
PHYLLOCACTUS GROUP

Only one illustration will accompany this chapter, in order to introduce for the first time in the series the genus *Heliocereus* Bgr. All species within this genus have somewhat slender trailing stems, of weak habit, with usually 3 or 4 angled stems, occasionally more, and finely spined. The diurnal flowers are mostly red in colour, unlike the variety we have included in colour *H. speciosus* var. *amecamensis*, which is white. Their flowers are all very similar in form to that of the illustrated variety, and range from 3 to 6 in (7.5 to 15 cm) in diameter.

All species are equally easy to grow and flower, given a soil containing a fairly high proportion of humus, which is always required for these epiphytic cacti.

Heliocereus speciosus var. amecamensis *Weing.*
(Mexico)

COLOUR: Pale green stems with yellowish to golden-brown spines.

SIZE: Shown at half natural size in Plate CCCLXXIV.

FLOWER: See Plate CCCLXXIV.

NOTE: This is an epiphytic species with 3- to 5-angled stems, which can sometimes reach up to 3 ft (1 m) in length. There can be up to 8 spines per areole, very fine, some of which exceed ½ in (1.25 cm) in length.

It is of easy culture, requiring a soil with a high proportion of humus, preferably about 4 to 1. It should be grown under shaded glass, otherwise stems can burn and requires plenty of water during the spring to autumn growing period. In the winter, a little water occasionally will prevent stems from shrivelling unduly, but a minimum temperature of 50°F (10°C) is advisable.

This variety was originally given specific status as *H. amecamensis* Heese, and is now grouped with three other varieties of *H. speciosus*. A number of epiphytic hybrid cacti have been produced using *Heliocereus* as one of the parents. These include ×*Heliochia* Rowley (*Heliocereus*×*Nopalxochia*), ×*Helioselenius* Rowley (*Heliocereus*×*Selenicereus*) and ×*Heliphyllum* Rowley (*Heliocereus*×*Epiphyllum*).

HATIORA AND RHIPSALIS GROUP

No further species are being described in this volume, but an index of the illustrations in the previous volumes is given below.

THE EXOTIC COLLECTION
Progress since 1966

Twelve years have elapsed since Volume IV was published, and in that time a further 3,000 species of succulents, including cacti of course, have been added to this collection.

Further species have been added amongst the Family Asclepiadaceae, including many fine Hoyas, some as yet unnamed, which provoke much comment from visiting subscribers to 'The Exotic Collection' monthly publication. Many of the Hoyas flower during two separate periods of the year, such that with a range of species grown here there are very few weeks in the year when at least one species is not in flower.

Reference was made in the Preface to certain cacti from Florida; in actual fact, a range of cacti and other succulent plants are now in cultivation here from that part of the U.S.A. We had been mystified for many years why the majority of species were seemingly not in cultivation anywhere, with the exception of *Acanthocereus* and the odd *Opuntia*. As a result of two visits to Florida, in 1973 and 1974, a range of differing species of *Opuntia* were brought back, some of which have already flowered and been identified, along with *Harrisias aboriginum*, *fragrans* and *simpsonii*, differing forms of *Acanthocereus pentagonus*, *Pilosocereus keyensis*, various Tillandsias, etc. let alone many other *Opuntia*.

One of the other sections of the collection which has been added to considerably is the Melocactus Group, with a range of *Discocacti*, *Melocacti*, *Buiningia*, etc. These cephalium-producing cacti mostly take many years to reach maturity and flower, but once they start, many flower non-stop from spring to late autumn. Some of our plants have produced cephaliums, so that we have been able to study their growth rates. Not a lot of information has been available to the amateur on these plants, particularly their culture, which requires a little more skill, but we have endeavoured to rectify this matter.

There are, in fact, many other cephalium- or pseudocephalium-bearing cacti in the Pilocereus Group, which have been only added to our collection in the last few years—such as *Austrocephalocereus dolichospermaticus* and *Pseudopilosocereus fulvilanatus*. Half-tone illustrations accompany this chapter of these very beautiful but relatively new species from Brazil. Both species have a quite bright blue epidermis, contrasting with golden-brown to reddish-brown spines and a ginger coloured pseudocephalium. These are not included in

View near the entrance to the main showhouse of 'The Exotic Collection', showing fine old *Mammillaria* clusters, plus climbing stems of *Selenicerei* up the post.

Two 6 ft (2 m) high specimens of *Pachypodium lamieri* grown here from seed sown in 1958.

this volume, as we may make a point of growing plants for a minimum of five years before writing about their cultural requirements.

During the last twelve years many of the South American cacti, seeds of which had been sown twenty, thirty or even forty years ago, have reached maturity and have flowered. Amongst others these

Austrocephalocereus dolichosper-maticus from Brazil, showing lateral cephalium.

Pseudopilosocereus fulvilanatus from Brazil, showing terminal cephalium.

include *Oreocereus* (*Morawetzia*) *doelzianus*, a massive clump grown from seed collected by Backeberg forty-seven years ago!! And yet it only started flowering in 1971. We have been well rewarded by the wait, as it usually flowers in early spring, mid-summer and again in the autumn. As with *Arrojadoa* such as *A. penicillata* (shown on page 1261), the stem grows through the terminal cephalium and then repeats the process later, often then flowering terminally as well as from the collar remains of the previous cephalium. If you refer to the illustration on page 1199 in Volume IV, you would see young *Oreocerei* and *Haageocerei*. Many of these are now 3–4 ft (1–1.3 m) high, and one particular specimen of *O. ritteri* has been flowering for the last four years, having been grown on its own roots for the entire period. This is in contrast to the same species shown grafted (page 1203 in Volume IV) which is now quite massive, but oddly enough has failed to flower.

We have also been experimenting with different types of plastic roofing for greenhouses, as a replacement for glass. In fact, as a result of this work, two of our houses are now roofed with corrugated 'Novolux', an I.C.I. product which has a ten-year clarity guarantee on it. This has been used for our experimental cold-house to such effect that many of the Opuntias, which always flowered reasonably well, have done even better. However, when used for a propagation house, this material requires far heavier shading than glass, otherwise young plants can easily burn.

A reference was made in Volume IV to the study of Hardy Cacti and Other Succulents and this has been continued with the building of a special raised alpine rockery for a range of species, mostly from North America, backed by a range of equally hardy North American Yuccas.

Tubs of tree-type Crassulas with Tradescantias in the foreground, which are placed outside in May, and returned to the greenhouse in October, before frosts commence.

FROST AND SNOW HARDY CACTI

In a climate like that of the British Isles, dampness in winter is a greater threat to many cacti, which in their native habitat in the U.S.A. and Canada endure much lower temperatures than in Britain. In fact, the lowest recorded here was in the 1962/63 winter when it did fall on the odd occasion to 0°F (−18°C), and remained below freezing day and night for three months! The plants which will be listed at the end of this chapter are those that safely endured those conditions. It is important to emphasise at this point that, when we refer to a species, there are some which have a very widespread distribution in the 'wild', such that only the form from the colder habitat can safely be grown in the open in Britain. When purchasing such plants, it is imperative that they come from a reputable and reliable firm which has this information.

Hardy cactus rockery shown in the summer, looking north, backed by *Phormium tenax* and Yuccas to the right.

Hardy cactus rockery under snow in the 1976/77 winter, looking south, backed by one of our fan-leaved Chusan Palms (*Trachycarpus fortunei* from a cold part of China) and Yuccas to the left.

In Britain, the main requirements for an alpine cactus rockery is a southerly or south-westerly aspect, preferably against a wall as it will be hotter in summer, and good drainage. It should be raised above the surrounding ground, preferably with a slight slope with 6 in (15 cm) or so of rocks and stone at the bottom. The soil mixture—if it can be called that—must be very poor indeed. The proportion of shingle and grit to humus will largely depend on the amount of rain which can be expected to fall during the winter months. We usually reckon on about 4–5 parts by volume of shingle, grit and sand to 1 of humus, plus a little slow-acting fertiliser, with about 1 in (2.5 cm) of shingle on top.

A rockery of this sort should be prepared in the late winter or very early spring, in order for it to be planted up with rooted specimens in May, once all frosts have passed. This will then allow the entire growing season in which the plants can become established. With such a well drained soil, you will find that watering will be needed during very hot weather. Please do not think that a mistake has been made by suggesting such a poor soil, as that sort of drainage is really important during the winter months. When it comes to some of the globular species, a little overhead protection can be given in very wet but cold areas. Yet provided the soil is correct and the plants correctly named, they should not come to any harm. Sometimes, as during the 1976/77 winter in Britain, when severe frosts alternated with rain, some Opuntias may become blotched. This usually shows in the spring. However, as specimens grow, very badly marked pads can be removed and can even be used for propagation purposes. With the onset of winter, your Opuntias will shrivel considerably and in many cases tend to lie down. This is quite normal, and it is only because they can do this that many of them survive.

A list of hardy cacti for the rockery (but not a complete list):

Opuntia compressa
Opuntia compressa var. macrorhiza
Opuntia cantabrigiensis
Opuntia drummondii
Opuntia fragilis
Opuntia juniperina
Opuntia polyacantha
Opuntia phaeacantha
Opuntia rhodantha
Opuntia rutila
Opuntia rafinesquei
Opuntia schweriniana
Neobesseya missouriensis
Echinocereus baileyi (northerly form)
Echinocereus viridiflorus
Echinocereus triglochidatus (northerly form)
Coryphantha vivipara
Pediocactus simpsonii (needs covering)

A list of hardy other succulents (also not a complete list):

Agave utahensis
Agave utahensis var. nevadensis
Agave parryi
Lewisia howellii and its hybrids * (also certain other species)
Sedum (wide range of species)
Sempervivum (wide range of species)

* Many Lewisias are grown as Alpine House Plants, but we have found that they do winter safely outside, with at the most a little overhead protection (such as a cloche).

INTRODUCTION TO THE
COLOUR PLATES

Every endeavour has been made to place them as near to the correct group, genus and species order as possible, as far as the arrangement of vertical or horizontal illustrations would allow.

Colour Plates CCXCV to CCCLXXIV on pages 1373–1398 belong to the Family Cactaceae.

CCXCV–CCXCVII belong to the Opuntia Group.

CCXCVIII–CCCXVI belong to the Cereus Group.

CCCXVII–CCCXX belong to the Pilocereus Group.

CCXXI–CCCXXIX and CCCXXXIII belong to the Echinopsis Group.

CCCXXX–CCCXXXII and CCCXXXIV–CCCXLIV belong to the Echinocactus Group.

CCCXLV–CCCLII belong to the Melocactus Group.

CCCLIII–CCCLXXIII belong to the Mammillaria Group.

CCCLXXIV belongs to the Epiphyllum and Phyllocactus Group.

CCCLXXV–CCCXCIV belongs to the 'Other Succulents' section of this volume.

CCXCV   *Opuntia microdasys* fa. *cristata* ($\times\frac{1}{12}$) (page 1229)

CCXCVI   *Opuntia rhodantha* ($\times\frac{1}{12}$) (page 1231)

CCXCVII   *Opuntia subterranea* (×2) (page 1232)

CCXCVIII   *Cephalocleistocactus ritteri* (×1½) (page 1236)

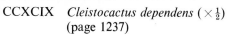

CCXCIX *Cleistocactus dependens* ($\times \frac{1}{2}$)
(page 1237)

CCC *Deamia testudo* ($\times \frac{1}{5}$)
(page 1238)

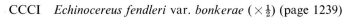

CCCI *Echinocereus fendleri* var. *bonkerae* ($\times \frac{1}{2}$) (page 1239)

CCCII   *Echinocereus gentryi* ($\times \frac{2}{3}$) (page 1240)

CCCIII   *Echinocereus papillosus* ($\times \frac{3}{4}$) (page 1240)

CCCIV   *Echinocereus grandis* ($\times \frac{1}{2}$) (page 1241)

CCCV   *Harrisia simpsonii* ($\times \frac{1}{3}$) (page 1245)

CCCVI   *Harrisia fragrans* ($\times \frac{1}{2}$) (page 1244)

CCCVII   *Hildewintera aureispina* ($\times\frac{1}{2}$) (page 1246)

CCCVIII   *Hylocereus cubensis* ($\times\frac{1}{4}$) (page 1247)

CCCIX   *Echinocereus melanocentrus* ($\times 1$) (page 1242)

CCCX   *Matucana crinifera* ($\times \frac{1}{2}$)
(page 1251)

CCCXI   *Matucana intertexta* ($\times 1$)
(page 1252)

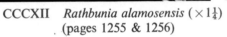

CCCXII *Rathbunia alamosensis* ($\times 1\frac{1}{4}$)
(pages 1255 & 1256)

CCCXIII *Rathbunia kerberi* ($\times \frac{1}{18}$)
(page 1257)

CCCXIV *Selenicereus grandiflorus* ($\times \frac{1}{4}$) (page 1258)

CCCXV   *Selenicereus urbanianus* ($\times\frac{1}{2}$) (page 1259)

CCCXVI   *Werckleocereus tonduzii* ($\times\frac{1}{2}$) (page 1259)

CCCXVII   *Arrojadoa penicillata* ($\times 2\frac{1}{2}$) (page 1261)

CCCXVIII *Haageocereus*
acranthus ($\times 1\frac{1}{2}$) (page 1264)

CCCXIX *Pilosocereus*
keyensis ($\times \frac{1}{25}$) (page 1265)

CCCXX *Pilosocereus*
lanuginosus ($\times \frac{1}{12}$) (page 1266)

CCCXXI *Sulcorebutia alba* ($\times 1\frac{1}{4}$)
(page 1276)

CCCXXII   *Acanthocalycium glaucum* ($\times \frac{1}{3}$) (page 1270)

CCCXXIII   *Lobivia hualfinensis* var. *fechseri* ($\times \frac{1}{2}$) (page 1271)

CCCXXIV   *Rebutia muscula* (×½) (page 1272)

CCCXXVI   *Sulcorebutia caniqueralii* (×1½) (page 1277)

CCCXXV   *Rebutia eos* (×⅔) (page 1276)

CCCXXVII   *Sulcorebutia rauschii* (×1½) (page 1275)

CCCXXVIII   *Sulcorebutia lepida* ($\times 1\frac{1}{2}$) (page 1278)

CCCXXIX   *Sulcorebutia tiraquensis* ($\times 1\frac{1}{4}$) (page 1278)

CCCXXX *Ferocactus emoryi* ($\times\frac{1}{30}$)
(page 1287)

CCCXXXI *Ferocactus stainesii* (large cluster) ($\times\frac{1}{40}$)
(page 1287)

CCCXXXII *Ferocactus stainesii* (close-up) ($\times\frac{1}{6}$) (page 1287)

CCCXXXIII *Sulcorebutia kruegeri* ($\times\frac{1}{3}$) (page 1277)

CCCXXXIV *Gymnocalycium horstii* ($\times\frac{2}{3}$) (page 1290)

CCCXXXV *Hamatocactus uncinatus* var. *wrightii* ($\times 1\frac{1}{2}$) (page 1292)

CCCXXXVI *Islaya krainziana* (×1½)
(page 1295)

CCCXXXVII *Islaya solitaria* (×
(page 1296)

CCCXXXVIII *Notocactus rutilans* (×⅔) (page 1300)

CCCXXXIX *Notocactus crassigibbus* ($\times \frac{2}{3}$) (page 1299)

CCCXLI *Thelocactus bicolor* ($\times \frac{1}{2}$) (page 1304)

CCCXL *Oroya peruviana* ($\times 1$) (page 1301)

CCCXLII *Thelocactus hexaedrophorus* ($\times \frac{3}{4}$) (page 1306)

CCCXLIII   *Thelocactus conothele* var. *aurantiacus* ($\times 1\frac{1}{4}$) (page 1307)

CCCXLIV   *Thelocactus nidulans* ($\times \frac{1}{2}$) (page 1307)

CCXLV *Buiningia brevicylindricus* ($\times \frac{2}{3}$) (page 312)

CCCXLVI *Buiningia purpureus* ($\times \frac{2}{3}$) (page 1313)

CCXLVII *Melocactus intortus* ($\times \frac{1}{2}$) (page 1322)

CCCXLVIII *Melocactus levitestatus* ($\times \frac{2}{3}$) (page 1323)

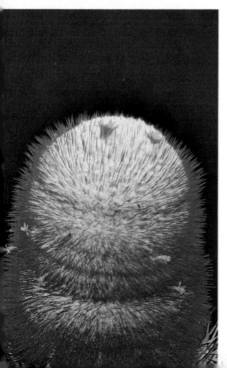

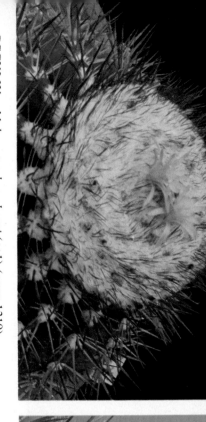

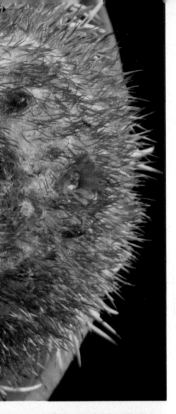

CCCXLIX *Melocactus broadwayi* (×1) (page 1319)

CCCLI *Melocactus matanzanus* (×½) (page 1326)

CCCL *Melocactus macracanthus* (×½) (page 1324)

CCCLII *Melocactus melocactoides* (×⅔) (page 1328)

CCCLIII *Coryphantha poselgeriana* ($\times \frac{2}{3}$) (page 1332

CCCLV *Mammillaria capensis* ($\times 1$) (page 1339)

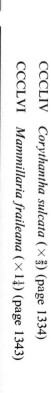

CCCLIV *Coryphantha sulcata* ($\times \frac{2}{3}$) (page 1334)

CCCLVI *Mammillaria fraileana* ($\times 1\frac{1}{4}$) (page 1343)

CCCLVII   *Escobaria
aguirreanus* ($\times 1\frac{1}{4}$) (page 1335)

CCCLIX   *Mammillaria boolii*
($\times 2$) (page 1338)

CCCLVIII   *Escobaria roseana*
($\times 1$) (page 1336)

CCCLX   *Mammillaria
estebanensis* ($\times \frac{2}{3}$) (page 1342)

CCCLXI   *Mammillaria goldii* ($\times \frac{3}{4}$) (page 1345)

CCCLXII   *Mammillaria longiflora* ($\times 2$) (page 1347)

CCCLXIII *Mammillaria guelzowiana* (form 1) (×1) (page 1346)

CCCLXV *Mammillaria louisae* (×1) (page 1348)

CCCLXIV *Mammillaria guelzowiana* (form 2) (×1) (page 1346)

CCCLXVI *Mammillaria saboae* (×1) (page 1354)

CCCLXVII *Mammillaria multidigitata* (×1) (page 1350)

CCCLXVIII *Mammillaria oliviae* (×1) (page 1351)

CCCLXIX *Mammillaria theresae* (×1¼) (page 1357)

CCCLXX *Mammillaria wrightii* (×2) (page 1358)

CCCLXXI *Mammillaria schumannii* (×1¼) (page 1355)

CCCLXXIII *Pelecyphora valdeziana* (×1¼) (page 1360)

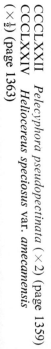

CCCLXXII *Pelecyphora pseudopectinata* (×2) (page 1359)

CCCLXXIV *Heliocereus speciosus* var. *amecamensis* (×½) (page 1363)

CCCLXXV *Brachystelma barberiae* ($\times\frac{1}{2}$) (page 1421)

CCCLXXVI *Ceropegia ampliata* ($\times 1\frac{2}{3}$) (page 1423)

CCCLXXVII *Ceropegia sandersonii* ($\times 1$) (page 1423)

CCCLXXVIII *Dudleya saxosa* ssp. *collomiae* ($\times\frac{2}{3}$) (page 1431)

CCCLXXIX   *Raphionacme galpinii* ($\times \frac{2}{3}$) (page 1449)

CCCLXXX   *Gerrardanthus macrorhiza* ($\times 4$) (page 1497)

CCCLXXXI   *Pachycormus discolor* ($\times \frac{1}{10}$) (page 1453)

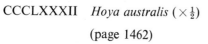

CCCLXXXII *Hoya australis* ($\times\frac{1}{2}$) CCCLXXXIII *Hoya bella* ($\times 1$)

(page 1462) (page 1463)

CCCLXXXIV *Hoya fusca-purpurea* ($\times 1$) (page 1465)

CCCLXXXV *Fouquieria macdougalii*
(×1/25) (page 1469)

CCCLXXXVI *Fouquieria splendens*
(×1/12) (page 1470)

CCCLXXXVII *Pachypodium densiflorum* (×1) (page 1487)

CCCLXXXVIII *Adenium·obesum* ssp. *multiflorum* ($\times\frac{1}{2}$) (page 1489)

CCCLXXXIX *Plumeria lutea* ($\times 1$) (page 1490)

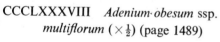

CCCXC x *Greenonium lambii* ($\times 1\frac{1}{4}$) (*flower*) (page 1474)

CCCXCI x *Greenonium lambii* (×⅕) (*in habitat*) (page 1474)

CCCXCIII *Stapelianthus decaryi* (×1¼) (page 1494)

CCCXCII *Edithcolea grandis* (×½) (page 1494)

CCCXCIV *Stultitia conjuncta* (×1) (page 1495)

Part Two

SUCCULENTS

OTHER THAN CACTI

List of Families to which the other succulent genera belong
(Volumes I–V)

Agavaceae   Endl.
 Agave, Manfreda, Sansevieria
Anacardiaceae   Lindl.
 Pachycormus
Apocynaceae   A. L. de Juss
 Adenium, Pachypodium, Plu-
 meria
Asclepiadaceae   R. Br.
 Brachystelma,   Caralluma,
 Ceropegia, Cynanchum, Decabe-
 lone,   Diplocyatha,   Duvalia,
 Echidnopsis, Edithcolea, Fockea,
 Hoodia, Hoya, Huernia, Huer-
 niopsis, Luckhoffia, Pectinaria,
 Piaranthus, Raphionacme, Sar-
 costemma, Stapelia, Stapelian-
 thus, Stultitia, Trichocaulon
Burseraceae   Kunth
 Bursera
Commelinaceae   R. Br.
 Cyanotis, Tradescantia
Compositae   Giseke
 Senecio (including *Kleinia*)
Crassulaceae   A. P. de Cand.
 Aeonium, Adromischus, Aichry-
 son,   Cotyledon,   Crassula,
 Dudleya, Echeveria, Graptopeta-
 lum, × *Greenonium, Greenovia,*
 Kalanchoe (including *Brvophyl-*
 lum), *Pachyphytum, Rochea,*
 Sedum
Cucurbitaceae   A. L. de Juss
 Gerrardanthus, Xerosycios
Didiereaceae   Drake & Castillo
 Alluaudia, Decaryia, Didierea

Dioscoreaceae   R. Br.
 Testudinaria
Euphorbiaceae   A. L. de Juss
 Euphorbia,   Jatropha,   Mona-
 denium,   Pedilanthus,   Syna-
 denium
Fouquieriaceae   A. P. de Cand.
 Fouquieria, Idria
Geraniaceae   A. L. de Juss
 Pelargonium, Sarcocanlon
Lobiatae   A. L. de Juss
 Plectranthus
Liliaceae   A. L. de Juss
 Aloe, Astroloba (was *Aprica*),
 Bowiea, Bulbine, Chamaealoe,
 Gasteria, Haworthia
Mesembryanthemaceae Herre & Volk
 Argyroderma,   Carruanthus,
 Cheiridopsis, Conophyllum, Con-
 ophytum,   Delosperma,   Didy-
 maotus, Dinteranthus, Faucaria,
 Fenestraria, Frithia, Gibbaeum,
 Glottiphyllum,   Imitaria,   Ken-
 sitia, Lapidaria, Lithops, Moni-
 laria, Ophthalmophyllum, Pleio-
 spilos, Psammophora, Rhine-
 phyllum,   Rimaria,   Sceletium,
 Schwantesia
Oxalicaceae   R. Br.
 Oxalis
Portulaceae   A. L. de Juss
 Anacampseros
Urticaceae   Link
 Dorstenia
Vitaceae   A. L. de Juss
 Cissus, Cyphostemma

AGAVE GROUP

A further two species of this genus are being included to add to the ten described and illustrated in Volumes II and III, plus introducing the genus *Manfreda*.

A. chrysoglossa is one of the lesser known species that does not reach immense proportions like *A. americana* does in its many forms. These smaller growing species make ideal tub plants no matter whether they are made of pottery, the lightweight asbestos/cement kind or even the thick pliable plastic ones. All species of *Agave*, without exception, are quite suitable for outdoor culture in tubs for the frost-free months, and many of them will stand cold frosty conditions if they are dry.

Visitors to 'The Exotic Collection' are able to see a variety of these growing in our experimental cold-house (unheated in winter), where they have been for the last thirty years, also others growing in the open-air which are covered with corrugated plastic frames for the winter months.

The genus *Manfreda* is one which some authorities amalgamate into *Agave*, but they are very distinctive plants with soft, often beautifully marked leaves and possessing a very fleshy succulent root system. They are easy plants to grow and if put in the open air for the frost-free months the leaves take on even brighter colours.

Agave chrysoglossa *I. M. Johnston*
(Mexico)

COLOUR: Fresh green leaves with brown horny margins, these changing to grey with age.

SIZE: Shown at just under half natural size.

FLOWER: Semi-pendulous flower-spike up to 9 ft (3 m) in length bearing numerous tubular pale-yellow flowers on the upper half.

NOTE: A somewhat slow growing species related to *A. bracteosa* which was included in Volume II.

A mature plant can eventually reach a diameter of 4½ ft (1.5 m), but it will take many years to reach such dimensions. As with *A. bracteosa* this species does not have fierce teeth along the leaf margins.

It is of easy growth, will do quite well in any reasonable soil, with plenty of water during the spring to autumn period. In winter it can be left dry, when it is quite safe down to 45°F (8°C), or even a little lower.

Agave utahensis fa. nuda   *Hort.*
(Nevada)

COLOUR: Fresh green to greenish-blue leaves with a matt surface, partly keeled on the under surfaces and brown to grey thorns at the tips.

SIZE: Shown at about two-thirds natural size.

FLOWER: Partially tubular yellow flowers forming part of an inflorescence on 6–12 ft (2–4 m) high flower spike.

NOTE: The type species *A. utahensis* is more akin to the illustration of *A. utahensis var. nevadensis* shown on page 728 in Volume III, in general appearance, possessing sharp thorns along the leaf margins.

It is very easy to grow and will eventually form into a cluster by means of suckers. It grows well in any reasonable soil with plenty of water during the spring to autumn period. In winter, it will stand many degrees of frost, provided it is completely dry, although in Britain with our damp winters, a very well drained soil is essential in order for it to succeed in the open ground.

Manfreda maculosa *Rose*
(S.E. Texas)

COLOUR: Pale green to green leaves with very variable brown to purplish-brown mottling.

SIZE: Shown at just above natural size.

FLOWER: Flower spike up to 3 ft (1 m) in height, bearing greenish-white flowers up to 2 in (5 cm) long which have a few very prominent stamens that stand out from the open flower.

NOTE: Many authorities have transferred the various species of *Manfreda* into the genus *Agave*, but we feel that the differences are sufficiently great to keep them separate under *Manfreda*.

It is a low growing species, having very soft leaves and teeth along the margins; it is produced from a tuberous rootstock. This rootstock will produce numerous rosettes and can soon colonise an area. In times of drought or fire, although the rosettes perish, new ones are soon produced once the rains come.

It is of easy culture, growing in virtually any reasonable soil, and enjoys plenty of water during the spring to autumn period. It can be grown equally well in full sun or under lightly shaded glass, provided it is given a big enough pot for the root system to develop properly. In winter, a minimum of 40°F (5°C) is quite sufficient, provided it is left dry.

ALOE GROUP

In this volume a further five species in this genus are being included to add to the 38 previously illustrated and described species.

Two of these species are miniatures from Madagascar—*Aloes descoingsii* and *rauhii*—the latter named after Professor Werner Rauh of Heidelberg, Germany, who has carried out many expeditions in various parts of the world, including a number to Madagascar. Succulent enthusiasts throughout the world owe a great deal to him for the many wonderful and often unusual succulents which he has introduced into cultivation over the last ten to twenty years.

Aloe sinkatana is a little known species from the Sudan, one of many new species described by the late Dr G. W. Reynolds, the author of two monographs—one on 'The Aloes of South Africa', the other on 'The Aloes of Tropical Africa and Madagascar'.

Finally, we have also included the very rare *Aloe polyphylla*, a protected species from Lesotho where it can be snow covered for part of the winter at 8,000 ft (2,650 m), up in the Phurumela Mountains.

Aloe descoingsii   *Reyn.*
(S. W. Madagascar)

COLOUR: Dull green leaves, somewhat rough surfaced, with off-white coloured markings and teeth along the leaf margins.

SIZE: Shown at nearly one and a half times natural size.

FLOWER: The flowers in this illustration are shown just prior to opening on a deliberately shortened flower spike, normally 6 in (15 cm) in height, varying from yellow or orange to even red in colour.

NOTE: It is a freely clustering species, with clumps made up of sometimes 100 heads, and yet the entire cluster does not exceed 12 in (30 cm) in diameter.

It grows well in a humus and sand mixture of about equal parts, grown under lightly shaded glass, with average watering from spring to autumn.

In winter, if left fairly dry, it is safe down to 45°F (8°C), unlike some of the other Malagasy succulents which require a higher minimum temperature for complete safety.

Aloe dinteri *Bgr.*
(Namibia)

COLOUR: Dark green to brownish-green leaves with white or cream coloured markings, and similar coloured leaf margins.

SIZE: Shown at just over one-third natural size.

FLOWER: Tubular rose-pink to almost white at the mouth, and just over 1 in (2.5 cm) long. Up to 40 of these are produced on an erect branched inflorescence similar to that of *A. sinkatana* (page 1415) and from 1½–2½ ft (50–80 cm) high.

NOTE: This is a fairly slow growing species related to the well known *A. variegata* and *A. sladeniana*, but usually remaining solitary and having leaves up to 12 in (30 cm) in length. The horny leaf margin has minute teeth.

In periods of drought, the very concave upper leaf surface allows it virtually to fold up and help reduce transpiration from the leaf surface.

It is quite an easy species to grow, but prefers a sandy humus soil mixture with slightly less than average water, unless the weather is exceptionally hot. In the winter, it should be left quite dry, when a minimum of 45°F (8°C) is quite sufficient, even lower if the atmospheric humidity is not high.

Aloe polyphylla   *Schoenl. ex Pill*
(Lesotho)

COLOUR: Pale green leaves with reddish-brown tips.

SIZE: Shown at about two-thirds natural size.

FLOWER: Inflorescence up to 18 in (50 cm) or more, bearing green tubular
flowers with purplish tips up to $1\frac{1}{2}$ in (3.75 cm) in length.

NOTE: This is quite a rare species from around 8,000 ft (2,6500 m) up on
the western slopes of Phurumela Mountain, some 48 km (30 miles) east of
Maseru, where at times it can be snow covered.

This slow growing species can be solitary, but more often than not it occurs
in clusters, each head eventually reaching a diameter of 2 ft (60 cm).

It grows well in a soil of about equal parts gritty sand and humus with average
watering during the spring to autumn period. In British winters, a minimum
temperature of 40°F (5°C) or even lower, if the atmospheric humidity is not
too high.

Aloe rauhii   *Reyn.*
(Madagascar)

COLOUR : Green to grey-green leaves with whitish markings and margins.

SIZE : Shown at just below natural size.

FLOWER : 8–12 in (20–30 cm) high, bearing 12 or more 1 in (2.5 cm) long, pink-red tubular flowers.

NOTE : This is a wonderful miniature, loose clustering species, where each rosette rarely exceeds 4 in (10 cm) in diameter, often much less.

This illustration was photographed in one of our raised beds in 'The Exotic Collection', where they have a free root-run but they still remain miniature in habit.

It is of easy culture, enjoying a little shade during the hottest months when they can have plenty of water. In cool weather less should be given, whilst in winter, provided they are dry, a minimum temperature of 45°F (8°C) is sufficient.

Aloe sinkatana   *Reyn.*
(Sudan)

COLOUR: Grey-green to green leaves with or without cream markings on the upper surfaces of the leaves, reddish tinged often in sun on leaf edges, particularly towards the tip.

SIZE: Shown at about one-quarter natural size.

FLOWER: Flower spike usually less than 3 ft (1 m), bearing small tubular orange-yellow to yellow flowers just under 1 in (2.5 cm) long.

NOTE: This stemless species usually clusters to a degree and carries as many as 16–20 leaves on a full-sized rosette. The under surface of a leaf is very rounded and is also spotted towards the basal end.

It is of easy culture given a reasonably well drained soil made up equally of humus, sand and loam, with average watering during the spring to autumn period, under lightly shaded glass. In winter, it can be left quite dry, when a minimum temperature of 45°F (8°C) is sufficient.

ANACAMPSEROS GROUP

No further species are being described in this volume, but an index of the illustrations in the previous volumes is given below.

CISSUS GROUP

No further species are being described in this volume, but an index of the illustrations in the previous volume is given below.

COTYLEDON GROUP

No further species are being described in this volume, but an index of the illustrations in the previous volumes is given below.

BOWIEA GROUP

The genus *Bulbine* belonging to the Family Liliaceae contains a great variety of mostly small growing herbs, some with succulent leaves, others with a tuberous caudex, whilst there are also non-succulent species.

Bulbine mesembryanthoides, which is included in this volume, is just one of over 30 little known succulent species. Some are rather uninteresting, but there are a number of species which are quite fascinating as they have mimicked other genera, such as *Bulbine alooides* Willd. (similar to Aloe), *Bulbine asphodeloides* Spreng. (similar to Asphodel) and *Bulbine haworthioides* B. Nord. (similar to Haworthia).

This genus has been studied by G. D. Rowley, B.Sc, of Reading University, England, such that he has prepared a very good Key to the genus, which can be seen on page 116 of the 'Lexicon of Succulent Plants' by Hermann Jacobsen.* The descriptions of some 30 varieties are to be found following this very useful Key to the genus *Bulbine* L.

HALF-TONE PLATE
Illustrated in Volume II
Bowiea volubilis   452

---

* 'Lexicon of Succulent Plants' Hermann Jacobsen. 1977. Blandford Press, Poole, Dorset, England.

Bulbine mesembryanthoides   *Haw.*
(L. Namaqualand, South Africa)

COLOUR: Succulent leaves are pale green, but much darker where they are translucent towards the tips.

SIZE: Shown at slightly above natural size.

FLOWER: The top part of a 6 in (15 cm) high flower spike is shown on the opposite page, the flowers being yellow in colour and very sweetly scented.

NOTE: A very unusual miniature succulent, where each plant has one or two of these very succulent leaves, produced from a tuberous caudex, and to a degree reminiscent of an *Ophthalmophyllum*, a genus within the Family Mesembryanthemaceae.

It is, however, easy growing, although relatively slow, requiring a sandy humus mixture, less than average water and growing best under lightly shaded glass.

Flower spike of *B. mesembryanthoides*.

The growing season is normally from the British autumn (September) through to the spring, when some water is needed, the flower spikes appearing around Christmas or the New Year usually. Although dormant during the hotter summer months, water has to be given to prevent the small succulent caudex beneath the ground from drying up.

In order that water can be given to the plants in a British winter when they are growing, an absolute minimum of 45°F (8°C) is essential.

CRASSULA GROUP

No further species are being described in this volume, but an index of the illustrations in the previous volumes is given below.

CYANOTIS GROUP

No further species are being described in this volume, but an index of the illustrations in the previous volume is given below.

CYNANCHUM AND SARCOSTEMMA GROUP

No further species are being described in this volume, but an index of the illustrations in the previous volume is given below.

CEROPEGIA GROUP

Eight species of *Ceropegia* have already been included in this series and a further two are being included this time, along with the introduction of another genus, *Brachystelma*, related to *Ceropegia* in the Family Asclepiadaceae.

There are many succulent Brachystelmas, either possessing a succulent caudex, as with *B. barberiae* and *B. modestum*, or having fleshy tuberous roots. The stems of these plants vary a lot, from short simple erect ones to the creeping and clambering kinds. The flowers have the same basic five-lobed appearance, some with the corolla lobes remaining joined at the tips, as with *B. barberiae*, and others opening out, as with *B. modestum*. Plants with succulent tendencies are to be found in many parts of Africa.

The two Ceropegias included this time have very uninteresting stems hence only colour pictures appearing of the flowers, both of which are quite large for this genus, around 2 in (5 cm) in length.

Brachystelma barberiae   *Harv. ex Hook. f.*

(E. Cape Province and Transkei)

COLOUR: Greyish-brown caudex and green leaves (produced later).

SIZE: Shown at half natural size in Plate CCLXXI.

FLOWER: See Plate CCCLXXV.

NOTE: This particular species is probably the most spectacular as far as its appearance and the objectionable smell of its flowers, akin to rotting fish! The flower cluster usually appears before the leaves and sometimes again after the plant is in leaf, some two months later. The leaves range from 3 to 4 in (7.5 to 10 cm) in length and up to ¾ in (2 cm) in width at the widest point, tapering towards the tips.

A rather sandy humus soil mixture is required for this species, also the caudex should be only planted just into the soil. Otherwise, if covered as it would be in nature, it may rot during the winter. Watering must always be rather light, and none in winter, when a minimum temperature of 45°F (8°C) is required.

Brachystelma modestum *R. A. Dyer*
(Natal)

COLOUR: Leaves and stems green or blue-green tinged with red, caudex is grey-brown.

SIZE: Shown at nearly two and a half times natural size.

FLOWER: White to pale cream with dark red to reddish-brown markings within the flower and corolla lobes.

NOTE: A very variable genus, because unlike *B. barberiae* (shown on the previous page) this one does not have its corolla lobes united at the tips.

It requires a sandy humus soil mixture, average watering from spring to autumn, when the short aerial stems appear from the caudex. This caudex should be put on the soil with gravel around it, as with *B. barberiae*, so that it does not remain too moist for too long a period. Best results are obtained under lightly shaded glass, but we have found that whereas in nature stems rarely exceed 2 in (5 cm) in length, in cultivation they can be three or four times that length.

In the winter, a minimum temperature of 45°F (8°C) is sufficient, provided it is left dry.

Ceropegia ampliata   *E. Mey*
(Transvaal and E. Cape Province)

COLOUR: Green stems with a small scale-like leaf at the node positions.

SIZE: Shown at nearly twice natural size in Plate CCCLXXVI.

FLOWER: See Plate CCCLXXVI.

NOTE: This is a very easy growing and free flowering species, which can be guaranteed to produce flowers from the node positions, often along the entire length of each stem. The stems are quite thin, often branching quite freely at the base as well as at intervals along their length, sometimes twining.

A soil of about equal parts humus and gritty sand suits this species very well, with plenty of water during the spring to autumn period, when it should be grown under shaded glass. Root room should not be stinted as it develops quite long, very succulent roots. In winter, it can be left dry, when a minimum temperature of 50°F (10°C) is preferred for best results, although most forms will stand lower temperatures.

Ceropegia sandersonii   *Hook. f.*
(Transvaal to Moçambique)

COLOUR: Green stems with small heart-shaped leaves of a similar colour and sometimes slightly blotched with pink or purple.

SIZE: Shown at natural size in Plate CCCLXXVII.

FLOWER: See Plate CCCLXXVII.

NOTE: This is a very spectacular species with its canopy appearance, but it is not quite so free flowering as *C. ampliata*, although it is equally easy to grow. The flowers as with most *Ceropegia* last for four or five days, in cool weather even longer. Stems, usually twining are slightly thicker than those of *C. ampliata*.

Cultural requirements as for *C. ampliata* except that it is a little more sensitive to cold, such that it can rot if the temperature falls below 50°F (10°C).

DORSTENIA GROUP

It is only in recent years that the succulent members of this genus have come into cultivation, but they have already proved very popular, particularly with those people who like unusual plants.

There are a wide range of species in this genus, native to many parts of Africa, Madagascar, India and even tropical America, but a great many of them are non-succulent. For the first time we are including three of the better known succulent species.

The flower structure is very unusual as you can see by the peculiarly lobed structures visible in the illustrations on pages 1425 and 1427 which are, in fact, inflorescences or, to be more correct, 'hypanthodiums'. These disc-like structures bear minute flowers without petals. In some cases, male and female flowers appear on the same hypanthodium. Each female flower, if successfully pollinated, will produce one seed which, incredible as it may seem, can be ejected when ripe over a distance of a few feet (a metre or so)! Fortunately, many of the species which are of interest to 'succulent enthusiasts' are self-fertile.

This genus was named after the German botanist Theodore Dorsten in 1737 and up to recently was included in the Family Moraceae, but is now in the Family Urticaceae.

Dorstenia foetida   *Schweinf.*
(S. Arabia)

COLOUR: Greenish-brown stems becoming grey with age, with glossy green leaves which have a slightly paler veining.

SIZE: Shown at about two-thirds natural size.

FLOWER: Pale green to a lemon-green colour.

NOTE: This is a very low growing plant, consisting of a flattened caudex bearing a number of erect or semi-erect stiff stems, which range from 1 to 2 in (2.5 to 5 cm) in length.

It is exceedingly free flowering, from spring through to autumn, as with most of the other succulent species in this genus. It enjoys a sandy humus soil mixture and should be grown under lightly shaded glass; it benefits from plenty of water during very hot weather, but less in any cool spells.

In winter it does not usually drop all its leaves, but can be left quite dry, when a minimum temperature of 50°F (10°C) is advised.

N.B. As mentioned on the previous page, the heading 'flower' is not strictly correct as the peculiarly lobed structures visible in the illustration are, in fact, inflorescences.

Dorstenia gigas *Schweinf.*
(Socotra and S. Arabia)

COLOUR: Greyish stems and caudex, and dark green to olive-green shiny leaves.

SIZE: Shown at about half natural size.

FLOWER: Similar to those of *D. foetida*, smaller and coloured.

NOTE: This species can eventually grow to over 3 ft (1 m) in height, but has a very thick basal stem or caudex up to 18 in (50 cm) in diameter. It is also the slowest growing of the three species we are including in this volume, but it is not difficult to grow.

Unlike the other two species, it is not so free flowering, but its cultivation requirements are exactly the same as for *D. foetida*. The leaves of this species have a somewhat shorter life than the others and is often completely leafless during the winter resting period.

This species can be propagated from cuttings, but they take rather longer to root—unlike cuttings of *D. hildebrandtii*, which are very quick to respond.

Dorstenia hildebrandtii *Engl.*
(Tanzania)

COLOUR: Very pale green stems and leaves.

SIZE: Shown at nearly twice natural size.

FLOWER: Green to purplish-green in colour.

NOTE: Unlike the previously described species, *D. hildebrandtii* only has a small caudex, which is partially submerged in the soil, bearing one or more stems up to 12 in (30 cm) in height.

It is also very free flowering from spring through to late autumn, or even into the winter if weather conditions are favourable. It enjoys a soil of about equal parts humus and sand, grows best in light shade, with plenty of water from spring to autumn, unless the weather is exceptionally cool. In winter, a minimum temperature of 50°F (10°C) is advised, and a little water.

ECHEVERIA GROUP

In this volume a further three species of *Dudleya* are being included, one of which, *D. saxosa ssp. collomiae*, is native to the Apache Trail region of Arizona, where it sometimes grows alongside *G. rusbyi* (illustrated on page 771 in Volume III). The majority of Dudleyas are to be found along the Pacific Coast, in the southern half of California southwards into Mexico and also on the islands in this region.

In cultivation, we have found that during very hot summer weather, greenhouse conditions can be too hot for them, even when partially shaded. This is true of many of the Canarian Aeoniums. Even in temperate climates, plants such as these will succeed better in the heat of summer outside in the garden, where a sunny position is then quite suitable.

Dudleya attenuata ssp. orcuttii   *Moran*
(Baja California and nearby islands)

COLOUR: Pale brown stems masked by the old dead leaves which remain attached. The linear fleshy leaves are chalky-green in colour.

SIZE: Shown at about half natural size.

FLOWER: Flower spike semi-erect up to 10 in (25 cm) in length, bearing a few small white or pink flowers with red lines and up to $\frac{1}{3}$ (8 mm) in length.

NOTE: This is one of a number of Dudleyas which branch quite freely, forming into dense clumps, but appearing rather untidy because of the mass of persistent dead leaves on the older parts of the stems. Such clumps can reach up to 12 in (30 cm) in height, in nature growing on sloping ground, cliff faces, etc., usually near the sea.

However, it is of easy culture, growing in any reasonable soil, with plenty of water during the warmer months from spring to autumn. When grown under glass it does not enjoy excessive heat above the 100°F (38°C) mark, such that we have had best results grown on the floor of the greenhouse or, better still, outside in the garden at that time of year. In winter, if left dry a minimum of 40°F (5°C) is quite sufficient.

Dudleya edulis *Moran*
(S.W. California, U.S.A., and N.W. Baja California)

COLOUR: Pale brown stems masked by dead leaf remains, whilst the leaves are pale green.

SIZE: Shown at just under natural size.

FLOWER: Flower spike up to 20 in (50 cm) in length, erect and branched, bearing many small white flowers.

NOTE Another branching species like the previous one in habit, rarely exceeding 6 in (15 cm) in height. In old specimens, the basal stem can be nearly 2 in (5 cm) in diameter.

It is of easy culture, requiring exactly the same treatment as *D. attenuata var. orcuttii*.

In habitat this species is known to hybridise freely with *D. blochmaniae* and *D. stolonifera*. We also found this species growing in association with *D. brittonii* and *D. attenuata ssp. orcuttii*, such that even further hybridisation is likely. *Echeveria* and *Dudleya* like *Aeonium*. *Aichryson* and *Greenovia* from the Canary Islands all belong to the Family Crassulaceae. Hybridisation is far more common in this family, not only between different species of a genus, but also between different genera.

Dudleya saxosa ssp. collomiae   *Moran*
(C. Arizona)

COLOUR: Pale chalky-green leaves.

SIZE: Shown at about natural size.

FLOWER: See Plate CCCLXXVIII (two-thirds natural size).

NOTE: This is a very lovely species, native to central Arizona and first seen by us on steeply sloping ground overlooking Canyon Lake on the Apache Trail.

It can produce leaves up to 6 in (15 cm) long and, being a fairly early flowerer in the spring, needs watering rather earlier than many species in the genus. It can in fact be grown in exactly the same way as the previous two species, but in the late winter transfer to a position where a minimum of 45°F (8°C) is possible, so that water can be given as the flower spikes start to appear. These can reach up to 12–18 in (30–50 cm) in length, usually semi-erect, and due to their weight later can break or even lie down.

EUPHORBIA GROUP

As in Volume IV, no additional genera are being included this time, but with the ever increasing interest in this genus and their availability, we are including three Monadeniums and ten more Euphorbias, all but one of which come from either East Africa or Rhodesia.

We do wish to extend our thanks to Mr P. R. O. Bally and Mrs Susan Holmes for their help, particularly in respect of the East African species, which they have been jointly studying for so many years.

It is only since about 1967 that some of the most attractive species of Euphorbias from Rhodesia have become better known, hence the inclusion this time of *E. griseola ssp. mashonica*, *E. wildii* and *E. memoralis*.

The majority of Euphorbias are relatively easy growing plants, provided it is possible to have two growing areas, one where the minimum winter temperature is around 40–45°F (5–8°C) and the other around 50–55°F (10–12°C). They are virtually pest-free plants in cultivation and differ far more in plant form than any other genus of plants.

Euphorbia ballyana *Rauh*
(Kenya)

COLOUR: Green to pale green stems with grey thorns.

SIZE: Shown at slightly above natural size.

FLOWER: Small, often three together, pink.

NOTE: This dwarf, freely branching species is of easy culture using a soil of about equal parts humus and sand, grown under lightly shaded glass in the hottest weather, when plenty of water can be given. In winter, however, a minimum temperature of 50°F (10°C) is advised in climates such as the British, where the atmospheric humidity can be high. In a better climate, where the winter humidity is low, a much lower temperature would be quite safe.

N.B. This species is not to be confused with *E. ballyi* Carter, also named after Peter R. O. Bally. However, that species is akin to a much larger triangular stemmed species from Somalia, *E. grandicornis* Goebel ex N. E. Brown.

Euphorbia burmannii var. karroensis
Boiss
(Cape Province)

COLOUR: Fresh green stems when young, changing to a whitish-grey with age. Tiny green leaves on new growth.

SIZE: Shown at just under natural size.

FLOWER: Produced at the tips of the stems about ⅓ in (less than 8 mm) in diameter, yellowish-green in colour.

NOTE: This slow growing variety is easy growing and will grow in any reasonable soil, but needs to be starved a little in order that the plant keeps its typical form. Because of this, use a relatively sandy growing medium and only average water, and do not re-pot too often. If this is done, or given free root-run conditions and too much water, stems will tend to straggle and become too elongated. In winter, it can be left dry and need only be kept just clear of freezing.

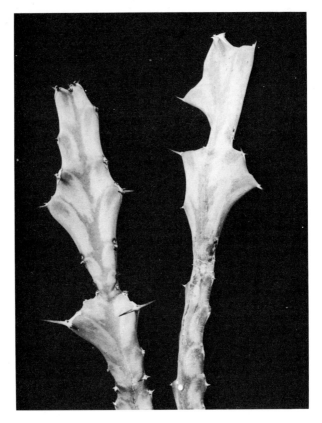

Euphorbia buruana *Pax*
(Uganda and Tanzania)

COLOUR: Green stems with paler mottled markings, thorn shields grey to grey-brown, thorns usually brown.

SIZE: Shown at approximately natural size.

FLOWER: Small, greenish brown.

NOTE: This is a far from common species in cultivation, but quite easy to grow. It is unusual in as much that the stems can sometimes be only 2-angled, otherwise 3-angled, these appearing from a subterranean succulent tap-root. The thorny stems can grow to as much as 2 ft (60 cm) in length, but usually much less than this.

A gritty sand and humus soil mixture is ideal, grown under lightly shaded glass in a deep pot, with average watering from spring to autumn. In winter, a minimum temperature of 50°F (10°C) is required, when a very occasional drop of water can be given, to prevent aerial stems from drying up.

Euphorbia graciliramea *Pax*
(Kenya)

COLOUR: Grey caudex beneath the numerous stems, which are in two shades of green and yellowish-green, with off-white thorns with dark tips when new.

SIZE: Shown at about half natural size.

FLOWER: Small shiny green flowers produced in pairs.

NOTE: This species can produce a very large flat-topped succulent caudex, from which numerous, often curved stems are produced, up to 6 in (15 cm) or so in length. The flowers are usually pleasantly scented, appearing during mid-summer.

In times of drought, in habitat, this species and its many relatives with an underground succulent caudex can lose all their aerial stems, but these quickly re-appear following rains.

In cultivation, a humus and gritty sand mixture suits it very well, with average watering from spring to autumn, under lightly shaded glass. In winter, a minimum of 50°F (10°C) is advised, when under damp atmosperic conditions specimens are best left dry. However, a little water can be given in better climates, but if a few stems partially die back, this is not serious.

Euphorbia griseola ssp. mashonica
Leach
(Rhodesia, Malawi and Moçambique)

COLOUR: Green stems, slightly mottled with reddish-brown thorn shields when new, changing to grey with age, forming a continuous horny border down each stem angle.

SIZE: Shown at about one-third natural size.

FLOWER: Very small as with most species, yellow.

NOTE: This variety can grow to over 10 ft (3.3 m). However, for those of you with limited space you can still grow this variety as a pot plant. The main stem can have from 9 to 12 angles, whereas the type species usually has fewer.

It is of easy culture, using a sand and humus mixture of about equal parts, but will accept many differing soils equally well. It needs plenty of water during the spring to autumn period, growing equally well under clear glass or when shaded.

In winter, it is best kept dry, with a minimum temperature of 50°F (10°C), although we have wintered some specimens down to 43°F (7°C) successfully, provided the atmospheric humidity has been equally low.

Euphorbia immersa *Bally & Carter*
(Somalia)

COLOUR: Chalky-green body and tails with off-white or grey thorns and thorn shield.

SIZE: Shown very slightly larger than natural size.

FLOWER: Very small, usually in pairs, yellow.

NOTE: A very miniature tuberous rooted species of very slow growth, only described as a new species relatively recently.

It requires a rather sandy humus soil mixture with less than average water from spring to autumn, extra only during long spells of very hot weather. Top-shelf treatment suits it well under lightly shaded glass.

In winter, it should remain dry, with a minimum temperature of 50°F (10°C), although where atmospheric humidity is low, it can safely take lower temperatures.

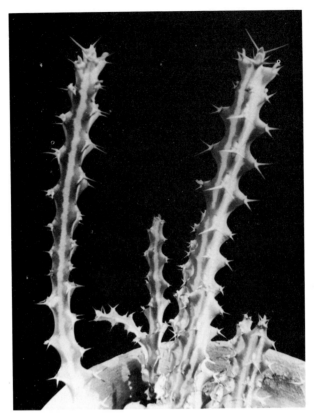

Euphorbia knuthii   *Pax*
(Moçambique and E. South Africa)

COLOUR: Pale green stems with a grey to cream stripes down each stem and light brown thorns.

SIZE: Shown at about natural size.

FLOWER: Very small, yellow.

NOTE: This is a rather attractive easy growing species, with a subterranean succulent caudex, from which arise numerous stems that rarely exceed 8 in (20 cm) in length. These have thorns in pairs, also tiny leaves on new growth, which dry up within a couple of months.

A gritty sand and humus mixture in equal parts suits this species very well, with plenty of water during the spring to autumn period, provided the weather is reasonably warm, and under lightly shaded glass. In winter, it should be left dry, when a minimum of 50°F (10°C) is usually required. Forms of this species from the Transvaal will usually stand rather cooler conditions in winter than those from Moçambique or even Natal.

Euphorbia memoralis *R. A. Dyer*
(Rhodesia)

COLOUR: Green to slightly chalky-green stems with brown thorns and a continuous grey horny margin on each stem angle.

SIZE: Shown at about two-thirds natural size.

FLOWER: In small clusters, yellow.

NOTE: The specimen illustrated is quite a young one, such that the central 5- to 7-angled stem is not visible. This can reach a height of 9 ft (3 m) or so, bearing branches that are 4-, 5- or 6-angled (as illustrated) and up to 3 ft (1 m) in length. When in growth small ¾ in (2 cm) long leaves appear on the new growth.

As with *E. griseola ssp. mashonica*, it is of easy culture, requiring fairly similar treatment but slightly less water. In winter, provided it is kept dry, it can be kept as low as 45°F (8°C), although in a damp winter climate a few degrees higher is safer.

Although this will eventually grow very large, it will take very many years for a pot-grown specimen to become too large for culture in a small greenhouse.

Euphorbia uhligiana   *Pax.*
(Tanzania)

COLOUR: Grey-green stems with grey thorn shields and thorns.

SIZE: Shown at about three-quarters natural size.

FLOWER: Small, green to greenish-brown.

NOTE: On page 793 in Volume III an illustration appeared of *E. uhligiana var. furcata*, showing the more symmetrical stem, compared with the type species illustrated above. This one eventually produces a large tuberous root and requires a sandy humus soil mixture. Average water, although extra can be given during exceptionally hot weather.

In winter, a minimum temperature of 50°F (10°C) is required, when it should be left fairly dry. However, in the latter half of the winter as the days get longer and greenhouse temperatures rise in the day-time, a little water may be necessary to prevent too many stems from drying up completely. They will regrow from the tuberous root, but it could take a couple of years for a plant to be back to its original size.

Euphorbia wildii   *Leach*
(Rhodesia)

COLOUR: Pale green stems and leaves.

SIZE: Shown at about one-third natural size.

FLOWER: Green, produced on a stalk up to 4 in (10 cm) long.

NOTE: This species can eventually reach a height of 9 ft (3 m) or so. Collectors with small greehouses should not be deterred by this, as pot-grown plants in this collection only develop quite slowly when compared with specimens under free root-run conditions.

It is of easy culture, in leaf from spring to autumn, when it likes plenty of water, grown in a humus and sand mixture of about equal parts under lightly shaded glass.

In winter, it is leafless and can be left quite dry, but a minimum temperature of 50°F (10°C) is advised.

Monadenium ellenbeckii var. caulopodium   *Bally.*
(Ethiopia and Kenya)

COLOUR: Fresh green stems and leaves.

SIZE: Shown at about half natural size.

FLOWER: Small yellowish-green hooded flowers less than ½ in (1.25 cm) in diameter.

NOTE: This is one of the easiest growing varieties, quite easily distinguishable from any other with the distinct longitudinally reticulate markings that characterise the stems. The type species can grow up to 3 ft (1 m) in height, but this variety tends to semi-sprawl and as a result is quite low growing.

A sand and humus mixture in equal parts with plenty of water during the warmer months suits this species well, although during the hottest weather it does best under lightly shaded glass.

In winter, it should be left dry, when most of the leaves will drop off as with some other species in this genus, and a minimum temperature of 50°F (10°C) is advised.

Monadenium magnificum   *E. A. Bruce*
(Tanzania)

COLOUR: Dark glossy-green leaves with paler veining, older leaves some-times tinged with reddish-purple; some of the prickles can also be similarly coloured. Stems paler coloured usually, gradually changing to brown with age.

SIZE: The illustration of the flowers is at about natural size, whereas the complete plant shown overleaf is at one-third natural size.

FLOWER: Peduncles are acutely angled, prickly green coloured or slightly reddish when flowered in Europe during the dull winter months, bearing reddish hooded flowers. The peduncles are normally red as well, when flowered in a better climate with brilliant light.

NOTE: This species is far from common in cultivation and two forms of it exist, the larger one being illustrated here and possessing much thicker stems. It grows as a branched shrub up to $4\frac{1}{2}$ ft (1.5 m) in height.

It is of easy culture, growing in any reasonable soil, with plenty of water during the spring to autumn period—when best results are obtained under lightly shaded glass and given free root-run conditions.

In winter, however, it should be kept dry, with an absolute minimum tempera-ture of 50°F (10°C). Some, if not all, of the leaves will drop off during the winter resting period. If it is kept at a much higher temperature in winter, a little water can be given very occasionally and this will ensure that the long lasting and unusual flowers develop properly, particularly when pot-grown. The flowers start to develop in late autumn and are often at their best in March, some three to four months later!

Monadenium magnificum *E. A. Bruce*

Monadenium reflexum   *Chiov*
(Ethiopia and Kenya)

COLOUR: Green stems tending to change to grey with age at the bases and green leaves.

SIZE: Shown very slightly enlarged above natural size.

FLOWER: Clearly visible in this illustration with the typical hooded formation (involucre), pale green in colour tinged with pink.

NOTE: This species is of columnar habit up to 14 in (35 cm) or so in height, sometimes solitary or sparingly branched, bearing these unusual recurved tubercles (somewhat like those of some of the deciduous Cotyledons such as *C. wallichii.*), and becoming even more downcurved with age. The leaves, which are quite short-lived with this species, are always curled up at the edges, as shown in this illustration.

It is not a difficult species to cultivate, doing well in a somewhat sandy humus soil mixture with about average watering from spring to autumn, under lightly shaded glass. In winter, it can remain dry and dormant, when a minimum temperature of 50°F (10°C) is advised.

FOCKEA GROUP

The genus *Fockea* was included in Volume IV and belongs to the Family Asclepiadaceae, as does *Raphionacme*, which is included for the first time. Fockeas and Raphionacmes produce large caudices from which the aerial stems appear.

Species of the genus *Raphionacme* are to be found in many parts of the southern half of Africa and also on the western side, northwards through Ghana to Senegal, just south of Morocco.

It is recorded that one caudex of *R. hirsuta* weighed over 6 lb (2.8 kg)! and can be compared with that produced by *Peniocereus greggii*, a member of the Family Cactaceae, although they can be much larger.

These plants are usually propagated from seed, but it will take many years to produce a large caudex. Our experiments with propagating *R. hirsuta* vegetatively from its perennial aerial stems have not so far proved very successful.

HALF-TONE PLATE
Illustrated in Volume IV
Fockea crispa   1104

Raphionacme galpinii *Schltr.*
(Transvaal)

COLOUR: Brown woody caudex, with green velvety stems and leaves.

SIZE: Shown at about natural size.

FLOWER: See Plate CCCLXXIX (two-thirds natural size).

NOTE: The caudex shown above is not fully grown as it can reach 6 in (15 cm) in length, bearing an erect stem or stems each year, which flower terminally as can be seen in Colour Plate CCCLXXIX.

It is of easy culture, provided a rather sandy humus soil mixture is used with slightly less than average water during the spring to autumn period. If the weather is exceptionally hot, extra water can be given. In habitat, the succulent caudex is completely submerged below soil level, but in cultivation in European type climates, it is advisable for the top half to remain above soil level, and to have a good layer of shingle or some other drainage material around it.

In winter, it should be left dry, when a minimum temperature of 45°F (8°C) is quite sufficient.

Raphionacme hirsuta *Dyer*
(South Africa)

COLOUR: Brownish woody caudex similar to that of *R. galpinii* with very slightly velvety greenish stems and green similarly surfaced leaves with pale veining.

SIZE Shown at slightly above natural size

FLOWER: Purplish flowers less than $\frac{1}{2}$ in (1.25 cm) in diameter.

NOTE: This species has a very similar caudex to that of *R. galpinii*, but produces a number of very long twining vine-like stems, which produce clusters of flowers in the leaf axil positions during the summer months.

Unlike *R. galpinii*, this species usually remains in leaf for the winter months, when plants can be left dry with a minimum temperature of 45°F (8°C). This species likes rather more water than *R. galpinii* and a soil containing a slightly greater amount of humus.

Most leaves tend to last for two or three years on average, although if the winter is mild and day-time temperatures are high, many leaves will dry up prematurely. To prevent this, a little water can be given occasionally.

BURSERA GROUP

The genus *Bursera*, belonging to the Family Burseraceae, contains a variety of tree-like plants native to tropical America, but only a few have any pretensions to being 'succulent'. One species is being included, *B. microphylla*, that is native to quite a wide area including the south-west part of the U.S.A. and southwards into the Sonoran region of Mexico. Despite their sometimes immense proportions, the trunks are made up of a very soft wood.

Plants such as these have become much more popular in recent years, often being compared with 'Bonsai Trees', except that the few succulent members naturally grow like this. The same also applies to *Pachycormus* detailed below, both of which possess the same common name, 'Elephant Tree'. (See page 1452, *Bursera microphylla*.)

PACHYCORMUS GROUP

The genus *Pachycormus* belongs to the Family Anacardiaceae and contains a number of interesting varieties native mainly to north-western Mexico, Baja California and some of the islands in the Gulf of California. As with *Bursera*, these also have a soft spongy wood texture beneath the bark. In its many forms *P. discolor* can grow in a more horizontal plane in a very contorted fashion, as can be seen in Plate CCCLXXXI photographed in 1976 by us north of San Carlos Bay, Sonora, Mexico. (See page 1453, *Pachycormus discolor*.)

Bursera microphylla *A. Gray*
(S.W. U.S.A. and Sonora, Mexico)

COLOUR: Stems reddish-brown when young, changing to grey or slate coloured with age, leaflets dark green.

SIZE: Shown at about two-thirds natural size.

FLOWER: Small in clusters, yellow.

NOTE: The illustration is of a fairly young specimen of the tree-like caudiciform, similar in some ways to *Pachycormus discolor* (overleaf). It can reach 24 ft (8 m) in height.

It is of easy culture and will grow in any reasonable soil, and after the seedling stage will grow in full sun. Some water is needed during summer months, when most plants are leafless, to prevent undue shrivelling. In winter, a minimum of 40°F (5°C) is sufficient, when water will be required occasionally to keep it in leaf. This type of succulent can respond to water at abnormal times and come into leaf.

Pachycormus discolor *Coville*
(Mexico)

COLOUR: Grey to grey-brown woody stems with a papery bark which tends to peel off in places and fresh green deciduous leaves.

SIZE: Shown at about half natural size.

FLOWER: Flowers produced together, small, varying from white or pink, even yellow.

NOTE: This is what is generally termed as a 'caudiciform'. It is, in fact, a succulent deciduous type of tree, which can eventually grow up to 12 ft (4 m) in height when very old (see Plate CCCLXXXI).

It is relatively slow growing, dormant and leafless during the hottest summer months and in Britain coming into growth leaf in autumn and remaining so until some time in the spring.

Cultural requirements as for *Bursera microphylla*.

HAWORTHIA GROUP

A further seven species of the genus *Haworthia* are included in this volume to add to the previous eleven. It includes a number of species which are now in general cultivation due to the efforts of the I.S.I. in California, an organisation which has done a great deal of valuable propagation work, so helping conservation.

H. reinwardtii has been included this time as well as the variety 'kaffirdriftensis' along with a special list of all of the described varieties of that species. We do not feel that most of these varietal names should stand, but in its many forms *H. reinwardtii* is a very attractive species of easy culture, most of which can be grown very easily as 'house plants'.

The only rarity that has been included is *H. sordida*, a very slow growing species, which is also very slow to propagate.

ADDITIONAL VARIETIES of H. reinwardtii and H. schuldtiana.

H. reinwardtii var. *adelaidensis* v. Poelln
H. reinwardtii var. *archibaldiae* v. Poelln
H. reinwardtii var. *bellula* G. G. Smith
H. reinwardtii var. *brevicula* G. G. Smith
H. reinwardtii var. *chalumnensis* G. G. Smith
H. reinwardtii var. *chalwinii* Res.
H. reinwardtii var. *committeesensis* G. G. Smith
H. reinwardtii var. *conspicua* v. Poelln
H. reinwardtii var. *diminuta* G. G. Smith
H. reinwardtii var. *fallax* v. Poelln
H. reinwardtii var. *grandicula* G. G. Smith
H. reinwardtii var. *huntsdriftensis* G. G. Smith
H. reinwardtii var. *major* Bak
H. reinwardtii var. *olivacea* G. G. Smith

H. reinwardtii var. *peddiensis* G. G. Smith
H. reinwardtii var. *riebeekensis* G. G. Smith
H. reinwardtii var. *tenuis* G. G. Smith
H. reinwardtii var. *triebneri* Res.
H. reinwardtii var. *valida* G. G. Smith
H. reinwardtii var. *zebrina* G. G. Smith
H. schuldtiana var. *erecta* Triebn & v. Poelln
H. schuldtiana var. *maculata* v. Poelln
H. schuldtiana var. *major* G. G. Smith
H. schuldtiana var. *robertsonensis* v. Poelln
H. schuldtiana var. *simplicior* v. Poelln
H. schuldtiana var. *sublaevis* v. Poelln
H. schuldtiana var. *subtuberculata* v. Poelln

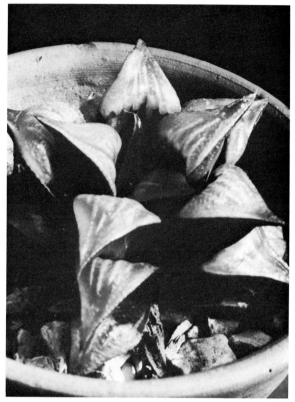

Haworthia badia   *v. Poelln*
(Cape Province)

COLOUR: Greenish-brown leaves with paler longitudinal lines on the semi-translucent parts.

SIZE: Shown at just above natural size.

FLOWER: Flower spike can reach 12 in (30 cm) in length, bearing 10 or more small tubular off-white flowers.

NOTE: A lovely dwarf, slow growing species, which often remains solitary, but one which is still far from common in collections at present. Its very distinctive appearance rates this species with other gems such as *H. maughanii, H. truncata, H. bolusii,* etc.

Unlike the quicker growing species, this one needs a somewhat better drained soil and should never be watered too freely for fear of rot starting around the neck of the plant.

Best results are obtained under partially shaded glass, whilst in winter it is quite safe down to 40°F (5°C) or even lower, provided it is left dry.

Haworthia pallida var. paynii *v. Poelln*
(Cape Province)

COLOUR: Dark green to slate-green leaves.

SIZE: Shown at about one and a half times natural size.

FLOWER: Flower spike rarely more than 6 in (15 cm) long, bearing a few small tubular creamy-white flowers.

NOTE: This miniature species can reach a diameter of 3 in (7.5 cm), but usually much less as it is a slow growing species. It usually remains solitary like the previously described species.

It is fairly easy to grow, but also requires a well drained soil and somewhat less than average water. Good drainage around the neck of the plant is important, as it literally grows flush with the soil as you can see (above). During the hotter months of the year it should be grown under partially shaded glass, whilst in winter it should be left quite dry, when a minimum of 40°F (5°C) is quite sufficient. A few degrees lower will do no harm to most *Haworthia*; in fact, there are many species which safely endure light frosts.

Haworthia reinwardtii　*Haw.*
(Cape Province)

COLOUR: Dark green leaves with small whitish (occasionally greenish) tubercles in 1 to 3 indistinct rows on the upper surface, many more on the lower surface.

SIZE: Shown at just below natural size.

FLOWER: Small creamy coloured flowers produced on a simple flower spike which appears from amongst the leaves near the top of a rosette.

NOTE: This is a very variable species, hence the long list of varieties on page 1454. It is, however, a very attractive and popular species of easy culture and one which will form into quite large clumps with rosettes up to 7 in (17.5 cm) or so in length.

As with the majority of species in this genus, it can grow in any reasonable soil. It also enjoys a certain degree of shade during the hotter months of the year. Although we would not suggest that all forms of *H. reinwardtii* are very frost-resistant, we have grown this species along with the variety *chalwinii*, *H. rigida* and *H. attenuata* in our unheated greenhouse where at times temperatures do drop to as low as 16°F (−9.5°C)!

Haworthia reinwardtii var. kaffirdriftensis *G. G. Smith*
(Peddie District of Cape Province)

COLOUR: Similar to the type species.

SIZE: Shown at about natural size.

FLOWER: Similar to the type species.

NOTE: This variety has slightly more tapering leaves than the type species, with 1–2 prominent lines and only a few white tubercles on the upper surfaces. The underside has pure white round tubercles in 5–8 indistinct longitudinal rows.

SPECIAL NOTE: *Haworthia reinwardtii* has a very lengthy list of varietal names, although we feel that many of them are not justified; but for those specialist collectors of this genus, we are listing all of them on page 1454.

Haworthia sampaiana *Res.*
(South Africa—origin unknown)

COLOUR: Brownish-green leaves with a slightly darker tip, tubercles usually only slightly paler than the actual leaf colour.

SIZE: Shown at about natural size.

FLOWER: Simple flower spike up to 10 in (25 cm) long, bearing the usual small creamy-white Haworthia flower.

NOTE: This species, which is of unknown origin, shows some resemblance to *H. coarctata* illustrated in Volume I (page 231).

The upper surface of a leaf is quite distinctly concave, with only a few small tubercles; the underside has the small tubercles usually in a zig-zag line.

It is of easy culture and clumps well, although the rosettes rarely exceed 4 in (10 cm) in height. Culture similar to that given for the previously described species. There is described a variety of this species (*var. broterana* Res. and Pinto Lopes) which has many more leaves in the make-up of each rosette, whilst the tubercles on the underside are larger and usually white.

Haworthia schuldtiana var. minor   *Triebn & v. Poelln*
(Cape Province)

COLOUR: Green to greenish-brown leaves bearing pointed tubercles of a similar colour.

SIZE: Shown at about natural size.

FLOWER: In this illustration the flower spike is visible, but had been deliberately shortened from its original length of about 5–6 in (12.5–15 cm).

NOTE: A very attractive little species, slowly clumping, but never one to become a nuisance by spreading too rapidly. It is, however, a species which requires somewhat better drainage, otherwise rotting can occur around the bases of the rosettes; so include additional sand and grit in the soil mixture.

Otherwise, treat as for *H. badia*.

SPECIAL NOTE: This species also has a lengthy list of varieties, which we are listing on page 1454 for the specialist collector:

Haworthia sordida   *Haw.*
(Cape Province)

COLOUR: Dark green to almost slate coloured leaves.

SIZE: Shown at about natural size.

FLOWER: Flower spike usually in excess of 6 in (15 cm), with the typical *Haworthia* creamy coloured flowers.

NOTE: This is probably one of the most desirable species after the ever popular species such as *H. truncata* and *H. maughanii*, but *H. sordida* is far rarer.

It is exceptionally slow growing for a species of Haworthia, requiring a rather sandy soil mixture and somewhat less than average water during the spring to autumn. It is only safe to give extra water during spells of very hot weather, but it does prefer staging culture under shaded glass.

In winter, it stands fairly cool conditions below 40°F (5°C), provided it is kept quite dry. Due to its rarity, we have not had the opportunity to experiment further with this species, despite the fact that we have been growing it here since 1965.

HOYA GROUP

Previous to this volume, only two species had been included in this series. As a genus they have not only gained in popularity in recent years, but a greater variety of kinds are more generally available to collectors.

They make ideal plants in a conservatory, the quicker growing twining species such as *H. australis* and *H. fusca-purpurea* appreciating free root-run conditions if available, whilst the others make ideal basket plants or can even be grown as house plants.

We cannot overemphasise the point already mentioned with *H. australis* regarding leaving the peduncles (flower stalks) on the plant. These peduncles elongate as the years go by, often flowering from the same one twice each year under ideal conditions, whilst the newer stems are producing new ones which often flower in their first year.

Mealy-bug does like most of the Hoyas, so keep a watch on your plants for this pest, although if regular preventative sprayings with insecticides are carried out two or three times each year, this pest should never raise its head.

HALF-TONE PLATE		COLOUR PLATE	
Illustrated in Volume III		Illustrated in Volume III	
Hoya longifolia	807	Hoya longifolia	753

HALF-TONE PLATE		COLOUR PLATE	
Illustrated in Volume IV		Illustrated in Volume IV	
Hoya carnosa	1108	Hoya carnosa	1151

HOYA GROUP

Hoya australis   *R. Br.*
(Australia)

COLOUR: Fresh green leaves, sometimes tinged with red on the centre rib position and even becoming bronzed over part of the leaf if in too much sun.

SIZE: Shown at half natural size in Plate CCCLXXXII.

FLOWER: See Plate CCCLXXXII.

NOTE: This is a very beautiful species with porcelain-like flowers, produced here during the latter part of the winter and again in the autumn, heavily scented particularly at night.

As with most species in this genus, the flower will usually last around three weeks, but do remember not to remove the peduncle (flower stalk), as further clusters of flowers will be produced from it for very many years.

Cultural requirements are much the same as for *H. bella*, except that a minimum temperature of 50°F (10°C) is advised, so that a little water can be given at intervals in the winter to prevent leaves drying up.

Hoya bella *Hook*
(Java)

COLOUR: Pale green leaves with a slightly purplish centre rib, whilst the stems vary from pale green to a pale purplish tinge.

SIZE: Shown at about two-thirds natural size.

FLOWER: See Plate CCCLXXXIII (natural size).

NOTE: This is really the miniature species in the genus and one that makes an ideal basket plant. Also, unlike its relatives, the flower clusters are produced terminally, then the stem branches afterwards.

The stems are very slightly pubescent (velvety); the leaves are convex and fleshy. It is a very easy growing plant, doing well in a soil of about equal parts humus and sand with plenty of water during the spring to autumn period. They should be grown under lightly shaded glass, otherwise (and this applies to most Hoyas) the leaves can burn quite easily under clear glass.

In the winter, it can be kept at 45°F (8°C), when for much of the winter it would have to be kept dry but some leaf fall can occur. Best results are obtained with a little higher minimum temperature so that occasional water can be given to prevent leaf fall.

Hoya carnosa cv. compacta *Hort.*
(Horticultural origin)

COLOUR: Dark shiny green leaves, the lower surfaces of the leaves much paler, velvety brownish-green stems.

SIZE: Shown at about half natural size.

FLOWER: Pale pink velvety petals, wine-red in the centre.

NOTE: This is quite slow growing compared with the type species, which we illustrated in Volume IV (page 1108 and in colour on page 1151).

This species does make an ideal basket plant, because of the compact formation of the stems and the contorted leaf formation which will then become pendant. It is of easy culture, requiring the same soil and watering requirements as the other species, but is less prone to leaf-drop in the winter if left dry at 45°F (8°C) as a minimum temperature.

There are other horticultural cultivars of *Hoya carnosa*, including *H. carnosa cv. marmorata* with yellow mottled leaves, and *H. carnosa cv. variegata* with a yellowish and red leaf margin.

Hoya fusca-purpurea *Bl.*
(Indonesia)

COLOUR: Fresh green leaves with silvery mottling, which increases as the leaves get older, stems live green and smooth.

SIZE: Shown at just under half natural size.

FLOWER: See Plate CCCLXIV (natural size).

NOTE: This is, we feel, one of the finest species, not only because of the large clusters of beautifully coloured flower that appear over many months of the spring and summer, but also because of the attractive foliage.

It is not a well known species in cultivation, but is now becoming more generally available, as it is not a slow grower once established. Provided it has just enough shade to prevent leaf burn, growth can be quite rapid during the spring to autumn period when it enjoys plentiful amounts of water.

The flowers do produce a great deal of nectar, somewhat more than most of the other species, so be on your guard against ordinary garden pests or even fungus spores, which can develop rapidly, causing sooty deposits on the leaves.

Cultural requirements otherwise as for *H. australis.*

IDRIA GROUP

In Volume II, an illustration of *Idria columnaris* was included, belonging to the Family Fouquieriaceae. In this volume we are including the genus *Fouquieria* for the first time, accompanied by illustrations of four of the eleven known species, all of which are native to Mexico. One of them, *F. splendens*, is the best known and this is also to be found through the south-western desert regions of the U.S.A.

The succulent Fouquierias have a number of interesting features, including a translucent waxy outer bark, which often peels off, allowing light to reach the tissues beneath. This feature is also shared by other caudiciform succulents including *Bursera* and *Pachycormus*, quite unrelated genera which are also included in this volume.

Whereas the monotypic genus *Idria* has always been sought after by collectors, it is only in recent years that the closely related Fouquierias have been wanted. A number of species have been made available to the amateur in plant form, and some have also appeared on seed lists as well. The papery seeds a little similar to those of the genus *Testudinaria*, germinate within a few days, and should be kept growing through the first winter by keeping them in a propagator where the temperature can be kept at around 70°F (21°C). If this is not done many seedlings can easily shrivel away, but once past this stage can safely cope with much cooler conditions in winter. In nature some species such as *F. splendens* safely withstand frosts and snow in the dormant period.

Colour photographs taken by us in habitat in Texas and in Mexico are also included in order to illustrate the appearance of adult specimens of *F. macdougalii* and *F. splendens*.

HALF-TONE PLATE
Illustrated in Volume II
Idria columnaris   504

Fouquieria diguetii *I.M.J.*
(Baja California and Sonora, Mexico)

COLOUR: Olive-brown stems with a corky or papery bark, which does peel off in places and become slate coloured with age. Bright green leaves up to 2 in (5 cm) long.

SIZE: Shown at just above natural size.

FLOWER: Flowers produced in panicles, scarlet, about 1 in (2.5 cm) long.

NOTE: This is the first of four species to be included in this volume, of which only eleven species are known. Only a section of a plant is illustrated. The largest specimens are to be found in Baja California, where they can reach a height of 25 ft (8 m).

It is not a quick growing species, but relatively easy to grow in a sand and humus soil of about equal parts, with plenty of water from spring to autumn when the plant will be in leaf. However, if it is left dry too long between watering the leaves will drop off, but new ones will soon appear once water is again applied. Once past the seedling stage, it grows equally well under lightly shaded glass or in full sun.

In winter, plants should be dry, when they are quite safe down to 45°F (8°C), or even a little lower.

Fouquieria purpusii   *T. Brand*
(Mexico)

COLOUR: Reddish-brown stems, but the swollen succulent basal trunk is grey-brown and corky, sometimes interspersed with patches of green tissue between, whilst the leaves when young are green, changing to purple when winter approaches.

SIZE: Shown at just over one-third natural size.

FLOWER: Flowers are borne in panicles terminally, creamy-white in colour and less than $\frac{1}{2}$ in (1.25 cm) in length.

NOTE: Although it takes many years for a plant to produce the swollen caudex—which can reach as much as 24 in (55 cm) in diameter, with stems up to 18 ft (6 m) or more in height—it is not a difficult species to grow. A soil of about equal parts sand and humus, and plenty of water from spring to autumn (assuming the weather is warm), will produce much quicker growth with the stems than you would see with some of the other species such as *F. diguetii* or *F. splendens*.

In winter, it should be left dry, the leaves having dropped off in the autumn, with a minimum temperature of 45°F (8°C).

Fouquieria macdougalii   *G. V. Nash*
(N.W. Mexico)

COLOUR: The stem is somewhat bronzed in colour, fairly smooth, peeling like paper in age, leaves green.

SIZE: Shown at about natural size.

FLOWER: Flowers produced in panicles of up to 20, each one about 1 in (2.5 cm) long and scarlet in colour.

NOTE: The above illustration depicts just the top 5 in (12.5 cm) or so of a two-headed 2 ft (60 cm) high specimen in our collection, in contrast to the 13 ft (4.3 m) high specimen photographed by us in habitat near Hermosillo in the state of Sonora, Mexico, (Plate CCCLXXXV). Some specimens of this species can reach up to 20 ft (8 m) in height.

This species branches sparingly near the base, but as you can see in the colour illustration, it branches very freely higher up; also, some of the branches become pendant.

In the wild, it will grow following rain, no matter at what time of the year it falls. Cultural requirements as for *F. diguetii*.

Fouquieria splendens   *Engelm.*
(S.W. U.S.A., Baja California and Sonora, Mexico)

COLOUR: Dark reddish-brown stems when new, greying with age as they change from a smooth surface to bark, with green leaves up to about 1–1¼ in (2.5–3 cm) in length.

SIZE: Shown at about one-eighth natural size.

FLOWER: See Plate CCCLXXXVI (one-twelfth natural size).

NOTE: This is the best known species of all, with a very widespread distribution from low altitudes up to 6,000 ft (2,000 m) in a few places. As a result, this species can range in height from only 3 ft (1 m) to 12 ft (4 m).

It has a somewhat candelabra formation, but the basal trunk can in old specimens reach a diameter of over 2 ft (60 cm).

Culture as for *F. diguetii.*

GASTERIA GROUP

No further species are being described in this volume, but an index of the illustrations in the previous volumes is given below.

KALANCHOE GROUP

No further species are being described in this volume, but an index of the illustrations in the previous volumes is given below.

KLEINIA GROUP

The genus *Kleinia* is very close to that of *Senecio*, such that in recent years it has been decided that all species under the genus name *Kleinia* should be transferred to *Senecio*. For these reasons we are listing below the species illustrated under *Kleinia* in previous volumes with their page number, but also the name changes where necessary.

MESEMBRYANTHEMUM GROUP

No further species are being described in this volume, but an index of the illustrations in the previous volumes is given below.

SEMPERVIVUM GROUP

A considerable variety of species within this group have been included in the previous four volumes, such that this time we are only introducing you to one of three natural inter-generic hybrids between *Greenovia* and *Aeonium*. These are now referred to as ×
Greenonium Rowley.

In addition to the half-tone close-up of one rosette, we are showing two colour plates, including a habitat one of the original plant photographed by Brian and Sally Lamb in May 1965, from which three cuttings were taken and brought back for 'The Exotic Collection'. It was found growing at about 6,000 ft (2,000 m) above Orotava, Tenerife, in association with *Greenovia aurea* and *Aeonium spathulatum*. *Greenovia aurea* was illustrated in Volume II on (page 533) and *Aeonium spathulatum* in Volume III (page 838). The other ×
Greenonium are:

    × *G. bramwellii* Rowley (*G. dodrentalis* × *A. spathulatum*) and
    × *G. rowleyi* Bramw. (*G. dodrentalis* × *A. haworthii*)

One other has been mentioned in literature as being between *G. aurea* × *A. glutinosum*. This could not occur in nature as *A. glutinosum* is native of the Portuguese island of Madeira, whereas *G. aurea* is native of Gran Canaria and Tenerife in the Spanish Canary Islands.

x **Greenonium lambii** *Voggenreiter*
(Tenerife, Canary Islands)

COLOUR: Brownish stems with bright green leaves.

SIZE: Shown at about natural size.

FLOWER: See Plate CCCXC ($1\frac{1}{4}$ times natural size).

NOTE: This inter-generic hybrid is very easy to grow in any reasonable soil, enjoying plenty of water during the spring to autumn period, when it is best grown outside in the garden in Britain. As with many of the related succulents from the Canary Islands, greenhouse temperatures can be too high, resulting in problems from such garden pests as 'green-fly' and 'black-fly', etc.

Its growing period is 'officially' in the winter from October to March, although the flowers usually appear during the early summer. During the winter months, it periodically needs a little water, when a minimum temperature of 45°F (8°C) (or even a little lower) is quite sufficient. The rosettes tend to open out in a flatter form when in growth, compared with the slightly more closed formation during the resting period as shown in colour in Plate CCCXC.

OTHONNA GROUP

No further species are being described in this volume, but an index of the illustrations in the previous volumes is given below.

HALF-TONE PLATE
Illustrated in Volume III

Othonna euphorbioides	842

HALF-TONE PLATES
Illustrated in Volume II

Oxalis gigantea	539
Oxalis gigantea	540

OXALIS GROUP

No further species are being described in this volume, but an index of the illustration in a previous volume is given below.

HALF-TONE PLATE
Illustrated in Volume IV

Othonna cacalioides	1155

PELARGONIUM GROUP

No further species are being described in this volume, but an index of the illustrations in the previous volumes is given below.

HALF-TONE PLATE
Illustrated in Volume I

Pelargonium tetragonum	275

HALF-TONE PLATES
Illustrated in Volume II

Pelargonium echinatum	544
Pelargonium ferulaceum	545
Pelargonium paradoxum	546

COLOUR PLATES
Illustrated in Volume II

Pelargonium echinatum	542
Pelargonium ferulaceum	542

PORTULACARIA GROUP

No further species are being described in this volume, but an index of the illustration in a previous volume is given below.

HALF-TONE PLATE
Illustrated in Volume III

Portulacaria afra	830

PEPEROMIA GROUP

No further species are being described in this volume, but an index of the illustration in a previous volume is given below.

SARCOCAULON GROUP

No further species are being described in this volume, but an index of the illustration in a previous volume is given below.

SEDUM GROUP

No further species are being described in this volume, but an index of the illustrations in previous volumes is given below.

TESTUDINARIA GROUP

No further species are being described in this volume, but an index of the illustrations in a previous volume is given below.

SENECIO GROUP

No further species are being described in this volume, but an index of the illustrations in the previous volumes is given below.

SANSEVIERIA GROUP

No further species are being described in this volume, but an index of the illustrations in previous volumes is given below.

SCILLA GROUP

No further species are being described in this volume, but an index of the illustration in a previous volume is given below.

TRADESCANTIA GROUP

No further species are being described in this volume, but an index of the illustration in a previous volume is given below.

COLEUS GROUP

Although the well known genus *Coleus* is not being included in this volume, there are a number of succulent members of it, which are not dissimilar from the species of *Plectranthus* which is illustrated on the opposite page.

They are mostly fairly small shrubby succulents belonging to the Family Labiatae, coming from tropical and subtropical parts of Asia, Africa and Australia. *P. prostratus* comes from the Kilimanjaro region of Tanzania in East Africa.

It is an exceedingly easy plant to propagate from cuttings or seed, and although shown as a pot plant, is also suitable for a hanging-basket.

COLEUS GROUP

Plectranthus prostratus *Gurke*
(Tanzania)

COLOUR: Pale green fleshy leaves with paler veining on the upper surfaces, often tinged with pink, whilst the lower surfaces tend to be more uniformly pink.

SIZE: Shown at nearly twice natural size (opposite).

FLOWER: Flowers produced on a short erect or semi-erect inflorescence, up to 2 in (5 cm) high, violet in colour.

NOTE: This is a very easy plant to grow, doing well in any reasonable soil. Once a suitable sized plant has been produced, one should tend to under-water it so that it colours up nicely.

In the winter, a minimum temperature of 50°F (10°C) is advised, when plants can be left fairly dry. If there is a tendency for some of the leaves to drop off, a little water can be given.

Plectranthus prostratus *Gurke*

DIDIEREA GROUP

It was only in the previous volume that this group first appeared, belonging to the Family Didiereaceae. So in addition to adding further species of *Alluaudia* and *Didierea*, we are including the genus *Decaryia* for the first time.

As with all the other members of this group so far included in this series, it also comes from Madagascar and is very popular with collectors who prefer the more unusual or weird forms of succulent plant-life.

Decaryia, as with most Alluaudias, can be easily propagated from cuttings during the spring and summer, drying them for about a week before planting into a sandy compost. This should be kept just moist with bottom heat and most species will root within four to six weeks. This can also be done with *D. trollii*, which propagates exceedingly easy by this method.

Seeds as yet are not generally available of these plants, such that only *D. madagascariensis* (Volume IV, page 1162) remains rare in collections, as that species has to be grown from seed.

HALF-TONE PLATES
Illustrated in Volume IV

Alluaudia comosa *Drake*
(Madagascar)

COLOUR: Stems greenish-brown to grey, with age, and green succulent leaves.

SIZE: Shown at about two-thirds natural size.

NOTE: This species comes in varying forms, such that their maximum height can vary from 3 to 30 ft (1 to 10 m), often with 4 or 5 main branches from which the smaller leaf-bearing twigs appear.

It is of easy culture, but even with small plants a deep pot is required, with plenty of water from spring to autumn, using a soil of about equal parts humus and gritty sand, under lightly shaded glass.

In the winter, it should be kept dry, when the leaves will drop off with a minimum temperature of 50° F (10°C). In warmer parts of the world, it can be kept in leaf all the year round, provided the temperature stays high enough so that it can be watered.

The specimen illustrated has been in our collection for about eight years and growth has been relatively slow.

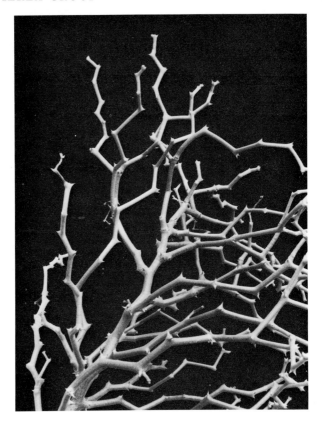

Decaryia madagascariensis *Choux*
(S.W. Madagascar)

COLOUR: Olive-green to pale brown stems.

SIZE: Shown at about half natural size.

NOTE: This unusual succulent will eventually grow into a thorny, but completely leafless, tree up to 20 ft (8 m) in height. However, this will take such a long time that this plant is quite suited to culture in a small greenhouse.

It is of easy culture, given any reasonably drained soil, but enjoys plenty of water during warm weather from spring to autumn, growing equally well in full sun or light shade.

In winter, provided it is kept dry, a minimum temperature of 50°F (10°C) is quite sufficient.

N.B. This genus is a monotypic one (just one species); also its growth is not fast even with free root-run conditions.

Didierea trollii *Capuron & Rauh*
(Madagascar)

COLOUR: Greenish-brown to grey stems and thorns, with green succulent leaves.

SIZE: Shown at just under natural size.

NOTE: Unlike *D. madagascariensis* which appeared in Volume IV (page 1162), this species is basically a horizontal grower. Only the end part of one of the stems is illustrated above, when in actual fact it can produce horizontally growing stems from its basal trunk, such that specimens can have a diameter of 6 ft (2 m) or more. These unusual bushes can attain a height eventually of 18 in (50 cm) as a tangled mass of branches.

It is of easy culture, somewhat quicker growing than *D. madagascariensis*, doing well in a soil of about equal parts humus and gritty sand, with plenty of water during warm weather in the spring to autumn period. It does not usually come into leaf until late spring, even though watering may have started six to eight weeks earlier. With the onset of winter, watering should cease and the plants be kept dry, with a minimum temperature of 50°F (10°C).

ADENIA GROUP

The genus *Adenia* belongs to the Family Passifloraceae (Passion Flower) and should not be confused with *Adenium*, which we have included in this volume in the Pachypodium Group, which belongs to the Family Apocynaceae.

Members of the genus *Adenia* are usually very succulent plants each possessing a thick caudex, from which numerous branches appear, sometimes stiff thorny ones or, in the case of *A. digitata*, slender ones equipped with tendrils.

This particular species cannot only be propagated from seed, but also from an aerial stem section which will later develop a caudex.

ADENIA GROUP

Adenia digitata *Engl.*
(Transvaal and Moçambique)

COLOUR: Dark-green caudex with purplish markings, below which there is a sort of grey rind between the darker part and soil level. Stems pale chalky blue with pinkish mottling and pale chalky blue-green leaves.

SIZE: (Above, opposite) Shown at natural size. (Below, opposite) Shown at half natural size.

FLOWER: Sweetly scented, nocturnal flowers; lemon coloured.

NOTE: This species is already proving popular because of its easy culture and free flowering habit, producing a number of aerial stems which will quickly cling to any supports by means of its tendrils.

A soil of about equal parts humus and gritty sand is ideal, with plenty of water during the spring to autumn period. In winter, it should be left dry, when a minimum temperature of 50°F (10°C) is advisable. Some of the stems will partially die back; this can only be avoided by keeping a higher winter temperature, when a little water can be given.

Adenia digitata *Engl.*

PACHYPODIUM GROUP

Previously, in Volumes III and IV, four species of *Pachypodium* had been included; to this we now add a further two, as well as introducing for the first time in this series two further genera, *Adenium* and *Plumeria*, which also belong to the Family Apocynaceae.

As with many of the Pachypodiums, such as *P. lamieri* and *P. geayi*, Adeniums and Plumerias grow either to shrub or tree-like proportions and are commonly cultivated as garden plants and trees in more tropical parts of the world. Plumerias, or 'Frangipani' as they are commonly called, are extensively used in their many colour forms in parks and gardens, producing large panicles of their heavily scented flowers. Oddly enough, few people have realised that these succulent trees are also suitable as 'house plants in much the same way as the common "Rubber Tree", but with the added bonus of flowers'.

Adeniums and Plumerias can both be propagated from cuttings, but they share with *Pachypodium* the sad fact that the seeds remain viable usually for only a few weeks. This is one of the reasons why they rarely appear on commercial seed lists.

HALF-TONE PLATES
Illustrated in Volume III

Pachypodium brevicaule	847
Pachypodium lamieri	848
Pachypodium namaquanum	849

HALF-TONE PLATES
Illustrated in Volume IV

Pachypodium succulentum
1166 and 1167

COLOUR PLATE
Illustrated in Volume IV

Pachypodium succulentum   1052

Pachypodium densiflorum   *Bak.*
(S.W. Madagascar)

COLOUR: Greyish-brown stem and thorns and bright green leaves.

SIZE: Shown at about one-quarter natural size.

FLOWER: See Plate CCCLXXXVII (natural size).

NOTE: This is one of the smaller growing species, compared with *P. geayi* shown overleaf, which grows eventually to tree-like proportions. In contrast, this one starts flowering usually when only 4–5 in (10–15 cm) in height, as soon as the base part of the stem really thickens up.

It is of easy culture, but far from quick growing and needs a slightly more porous soil mixture than the larger and quicker growing species. It comes into growth and leaf in the spring through to the autumn, but can only be watered fairly freely during the warmer weather. In winter, it should be kept dry, when a minimum temperature of 50°F (10°C) is advised.

Pachypodium geayi *Cost. et Bois*
(S.W. Madagascar)

COLOUR: Greyish-brown stem, with somewhat paler thorns and dark green leaves with rather shiny upper surfaces.

SIZE: Shown about half natural size.

FLOWER: White, slightly under $\frac{3}{4}$ in (2 cm) in length, produced as a rather lax inflorescence.

NOTE: This is a very easy growing species, one which will eventually reach up to 20 ft (8 m) in height as an erect tree and normally unbranched, in contrast to the young specimen shown above, which branched as a seedling.

It enjoys a soil of about equal parts humus and sand, with plenty of water during warmer weather in the spring to autumn period. As with most of the Madagascan members of this genus, it is usually leafless through the winter months when it is kept dry. In that period, a minimum temperature of 50°F (10°C) is advised.

N.B. This particular species is very suited to culture indoors as a house plant, particularly in warm, centrally heated homes. When grown in this way, it will need water in the winter and will remain in leaf.

Adenium obesum ssp. multiflorum   *Codd.*
(Transvaal and Rhodesia)

COLOUR: Greenish-brown stems changing to grey towards the swollen base, and glossy green leaves with pale midribs.

SIZE: Shown at just over one-third natural size.

FLOWER: See Plate CCCLXXXVIII (half natural size).

NOTE: This species does not usually flower until it has reached about 8 in (20 cm) in height). It can eventually grow to 6 ft (2 m), with numerous multi-branched stems.

It is an easy growing plant that likes a soil of about equal parts of humus and gritty sand, grown under lightly shaded glass with plenty of water during the spring to autumn period, provided the weather is warm. In the winter, however, plants are safe down to about 55°F (12°C), when they should be kept dry and when they will lose most if not all of their leaves.

This plant is also referred to as *A. multiflorum* Klotsch.

Plumeria rubra *L.*
(Mexico to Venezuela)

COLOUR: Olive-green to brown stems, greying with age, with fresh green leaves that have a paler midrib and veining.

SIZE: Shown at about half natural size.

FLOWER: Similar to *P. lutea* (Plate CCCLXXXIX) but red with a yellow throat, produced as a large inflorescence.

NOTE: This is just the top of a young single-stemmed plant only 2 ft (60 cm) high, which will in time develop into a large multi-branched tree. The highly scented flowers are produced terminally such that the stems branch at that position later on, usually at the start of the following spring.

Although these will eventually grow large, they are quite suitable for pot or tub culture and for use as house plants. They will grow in any reasonable soil, but require plenty of water throughout the spring to autumn period. When grown in the greenhouse, lightly shaded glass is preferable to prevent leaf burn, but this does not apply in the open air.

In the winter, it is quite safe down to 50°F (10°C), when it should be kept dry, but a little water can be given in mild weather to prevent the stems from wrinkling through dryness. At this time of year all the leaves will drop off.

FOOTNOTE: Colour Plate CCCLXXXIX (at natural size) depicts just a few flowers of *Plumeria lutea* Ruiz & Pav., probably the commonest species of all. Its habit and cultural requirements are the same as for *P. rubra*.

STAPELIAD GROUP

This group has already been well covered in Volumes I to IV, such that here we are only including a further four species, including three more genera—*Edithcolea, Stapelianthus* and *Stultitia*. It has been a very difficult decision to take, particularly as we could have included colour plates of such genera as *Rhitidocaulon, Pseudolithos*, etc. However, at present, these species are so rare in cultivation that very few collectors will have the opportunity of growing them for many years to come. In fact, *Pseudolithos* is an extremely difficult genus to grow in cultivation, no matter whether it is on its own roots or grafted.

Edithcolea, although a difficult species to grow, is available, and even if a plant collapses in cultivation, it is usually possible to save a few sections of stems, and relatively quickly grow another fine plant to flowering size within twelve months. The patterning on the flower of *E. grandis* varies considerably, as do many other Stapeliads.

Species of *Stapelianthus* have been readily available for many years, as have some of the Stultitias in the last ten years or so. We feel that *S. conjuncta* rivals many of the ever popular *Huernia* for flower structure and beauty, with its very distinctive raised annulus, reminiscent of some of the 'lifebuoy' *Huernia*.

Indian Stapeliads are not so well known in cultivation, with perhaps the exception of *Frerea indica* illustrated in Volume III (page 886). Some of them like *Edithcolea*, do present some problems in cultivation. However, they are exceedingly free flowering, as one can see by the unusual terminal flowered *Caralluma pauciflora*. Species such as these are a challenge in cultivation, particularly for those of us living in countries where the atmospheric humidity is high in the cold winter months.

Caralluma pauciflora *N. E. Br.*
(India)

COLOUR: Pale green stems often tinged with brown in sun.

SIZE: Shown at just above natural size.

FLOWER: About 1 in (2.5 cm) in diameter, cream with brown transverse markings.

NOTE: It is not easy to grow in a climate such as that of Britain, where there is high humidity in winter; thus a rather sandy humus soil mixture is required. It grows best under lightly shaded glass with less than average water from spring to autumn, unless the weather is very hot, when extra can be given.

In winter, however, they should be kept dry, particularly if a minimum of only 50°F (10°C) is maintained and preferably somewhat higher. Regular spraying or watering with Chinosol (potassium hydroxyquinoline sulphate) is essential to keep this type of Stapeliad free from 'Black Rot.

1493

Edithcolea grandis *N. E. Br.*
(Kenya, Socotra and Somalia)

COLOUR: Olive-green stems often tinged with bronze or purple.

SIZE: Shown at about half natural size in Plate CCCXCII.

FLOWER: See Plate CCCXCII.

NOTE: This is a very beautiful member of this group, but it does present somewhat of a 'challenge to cultivate it successfully, even in more tropical climates. This is due to the fact that it is more prone to 'Black Rot'. The regular use of a drench of Chinosol solution (potassium hydroxyquinoline sulphate) is essential at least three times during the growing season.

The stems of this species may reach 12 in (30 cm) in height, branching very freely and possessing very sharp teeth. A sandy humus soil mixture is required, with somewhat less than average water—except in very hot weather when it enjoys extra—and grown under lightly shaded glass, when it can flower very freely. During the winter months, it should be left dry and never allowed to endure temperatures lower than 50°F (10°C). If kept at about 70°F (21°C) in the winter, a little water, sufficient only to prevent shrivelling, with Chinosol added can be given very occasionally.

Stapelianthus decaryi *Choux*
(Madagascar)

COLOUR: Purplish-green mottled stems.

SIZE: Shown at just above natural size in Plate CCCXCIII.

FLOWER: See Plate CCCXCIII.

NOTE: This is a very densely clustering species with stems that can reach 4 in (10 cm) in length, but are usually only half that size. The stems are very slim, just ⅓ in (8 mm) in diameter.

Although this is quite an easy growing species, it is not as free flowering as the other Stapeliads illustrated in this volume. Its cultural requirements are much the same as for *Edithcolea grandis*, although it is not so prone to 'Black Rot'.

A closely related species to this one, also from Madagascar, is *S. madagascariensis*, which has very similar stems but has shorter tubed flowers.

Stultitia conjuncta *White & Sloane*
(Transvaal)

COLOUR: Bluish-green stems with purplish markings.

SIZE: Shown at about natural size in Plate CCCXCIV.

FLOWER: See Plate CCCXCIV.

NOTE: This is a prostrate growing species, often producing subterranean stems, but they rarely exceed 3 in (7.5 cm) in length. They are usually 4-angled but occasionally 5 angled.

It is a fairly easy growing species, provided a rather sandy humus soil mixture is used. Slightly less than average water is needed, unless the weather is very hot, when extra can be given. It grows best under lightly shaded glass and should be provided with a wide but quite shallow pan, when specimens will develop properly. In winter, it should be kept fairly dry, only a little water being needed very occasionally to prevent shrivelling, when a minimum temperature of 50°F (10°C) is advised in a damp climate. In countries with low humidity in winter, this species can be kept quite safely at a lower temperature.

FOOTNOTE: The genus *Stultitia* was first erected in 1933, and for many years included just two species; *S. cooperi.* Phillips and *S. tapscottii.* Phillips. Since then, a further five species have been added including this one from the Transvaal. In addition to *S. hardyii* from the same province, the others come from Cape Province, Natal, Botswana and Rhodesia. All of them have this prominent raised annulus, and deeply divided outer corona lobes, previously certain species had been listed under *Stapelia* and *Stapeliopsis.*

XEROSICYOS GROUP

Although *Gerrardanthus macrorhizus* belongs to the same Family (Cucurbitaceae) as *Xerosicyos perrieri*, which was illustrated in Volume III (page 885), they are totally different plants in appearance with the exception of their basic flower structure and the fact that their stems both have tendrils.

The stems of the *Gerrardanthus* are produced annually from a huge succulent caudex, whereas those of *Xerosicyos perrieri* are perennial and exceedingly easy to propagate from cuttings.

G. macrorhizus is one of two species to be found in collections, the other is *G. lobatus. C. Jeffrey* comes from West, Central and East Africa.

HALF-TONE PLATE
Illustrated in Volume III
Xerosicyos perrieri   885

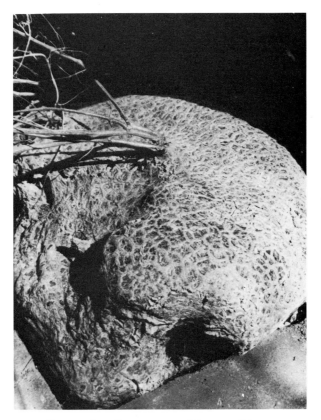

Gerrardanthus macrorhizus *Harv.*
(South and East Africa)

COLOUR: Grey to greyish-brown mottled caudex with green stems and leaves.

SIZE: Shown at about one-fifth natural size.

FLOWER: See Plate CCCLXXX (four times natural size).

NOTE: This species can produce relatively rapidly a quite large caudex up to 2 ft (60 cm) or more in diameter. Sometimes the caudex is rather flattened as shown, but is usually more dome-shaped. The basal stem or stems become woody after a few years, but much of the very long stems produced complete with tendrils dry up with the approach of winter, when watering is stopped. These stems can grow 15 ft (5 m) in a matter of a few months each year, flowering very freely from mid-summer onwards.

It is best grown on the surface of sandy humus soil mixture, with plenty of water and under lightly shaded glass during the spring to autumn period. In winter, it should be kept dry, with a minimum temperature of 45°F (8°C), or a little higher if the atmospheric humidity is also high.

THE EXOTIC COLLECTION

Slim white stems of *Cephalocleistocactus ritteri* and other species of *Trichocerei* at the main entrance to 'The Exotic Collection'.

THE EXOTIC COLLECTION under the personal direction of Edgar Lamb and Brian M. Lamb, 16–18 Franklin Road, WORTHING, Sussex BN13 2 PQ, England, publishes a *monthly colour publication* on an annual subscription of £4.50 *for the U.K. or* $10.00 (*U.S.A.*) *for overseas subscribers.* You receive at least *72 pages of full colour illustrations*, plus articles, including 24 Reference Plates per year which by means of their unique numbering system build into a loose-leaf *colour encyclopaedia* of illustrations accompanied by cultural information. *Named seeds* and *plant lists* are sent to subscribers in all parts of the world. Subscriptions operate on a January to December basis.

INDEX TO GENERA, VOLUMES I–V

(Species within each genus appear alphabetically)

	Vol. I Page	Vol. II Page	Vol. III Page	Vol. IV Page	Vol. V Page
Leuchtenbergia	—	—	655	—	—
Lithops	258	—	822	1132	—
Lobivia	85	371	628	953	1271
Lophocereus	74	—	—	—	—
Lophophora	111	—	—	—	1297
Luckhoffia	—	—	—	1191	—
Machaerocereus	—	353	—	—	—
Maihuenia	—	329	—	—	—
Malacocarpus (now *Wigginsia*)	112	—	660	981	—
Mamillopsis	—	404	—	—	—
Mammillaria	127	402	692	1016	1337
Manfreda	—	—	—	—	1409
Matucana	—	—	—	935	1251
Mediolobia (now *Rebutia*)	89	—	—	954	—
Melocactus	—	—	661	—	1318
Mila	—	—	662	—	—
Monadenium	—	494	—	1100	1444
Monanthes	—	536	—	1153	—
Monilaria	—	521	—	1144	—
Monvillea	—	—	610	—	—
Myrtillocactus	53	—	—	—	—
Nananthus	—	522	—	—	—
Neobesseya	—	—	—	1029	—
Neogomesia	—	—	—	982	—
Neohenricia	—	518	—	—	—
Neolloydia	—	—	—	1030	—
Neoporteria	—	—	666	983	—
Nopalxochia	156	—	—	—	—
Notocactus	113	—	659	990	1299
Nyctocereus	54	—	—	—	—
Obregonia	—	—	663	—	—
Ophthalmophyllum	—	527	824	1145	—
Opuntia	22	330	599	912	1229
Oreocereus	79	360	—	941	—
Oroya	—	—	—	—	1301
Othonna	—	—	842	1155	—
Oxalis	—	539	—	—	—
Pachycereus	55	—	—	—	1253
Pachycormus	—	—	—	—	1453
Pachyphytum	191	472	772	—	—
Pachypodium	—	—	847	1166	1487
Parodia	121	—	664	991	—
Pectinaria	—	—	878	—	—
Pediocactus	—	—	—	992	—
Pedilanthus	225	—	—	—	—
Pelargonium	274	554	—	—	—
Pelecyphora	—	404	—	—	1359
Peperomia	—	548	—	—	—
Pereskia	—	—	596	—	—
Pereskiopsis	—	—	—	—	1226
Pfeiffera	159	—	—	—	—
Phyllocactus	—	414	—	—	—
Piaranthus	—	—	879	—	—
Pilosocereus (see also *Cephalocereus*)	—	—	—	—	1265
Plectranthus	—	—	—	—	1478
Pleiospilos	—	527	827	—	—

	Vol. I Page	Vol. II Page	Vol. III Page	Vol. IV Page	Vol. V Page
Plumeria	—	—	—	—	1490
Porfiria	—	—	—	1032	—
Portulacaria	—	—	830	—	—
Psammophora	—	—	845	—	—
Pterocactus	—	338	—	—	—
Pyrrhocactus	—	—	665	—	—
Quiabentia	—	339	—	—	1228
Raphionacme	—	—	—	—	1449
Rathbunia	—	—	—	—	1255
Rebutia	90	368	630	957	1272
Rhinephyllum	—	518	—	—	—
Rhipsalidopsis	—	414	—	—	—
Rhipsalis	160	420	—	—	—
Rimaria	264	—	—	—	—
Rochea (now *Crassula*)	—	—	—	1076	—
Sansevieria	—	—	853	1173	—
Sarcocaulon	—	550	—	—	—
Sarcostemma	—	—	763	—	—
Sceletium	—	—	—	1146	—
Schlumbergera	—	418	—	—	—
Schwantesia	—	—	828	—	—
Scilla	—	—	—	1181	—
Sclerocactus	—	—	668	—	—
Sedum	277	552	—	1053	—
Selenicereus	—	354	—	—	1258
Senecio	279	558	—	1171	—
Solisia	—	—	—	—	1361
Stapelia	294	—	880	1201	—
Stapelianthus	—	—	—	—	1494
Stenocactus	—	392	669	997	—
Stephanocereus	—	—	—	—	1267
Stetsonia	—	355	—	—	—
Strombocactus	—	377	—	—	—
Stultitia	—	—	—	—	1495
Sulcorebutia	—	—	—	—	1274
Synadenium	—	—	796	—	—
Tacinga	—	—	597	—	—
Tavaresia	—	—	—	1193	—
Testudinaria	—	565	—	—	—
Thelocactus	—	—	672	—	1304
Thrixanthocereus	—	—	—	946	—
Toumeya	—	397	673	1001	—
Tradescantia	—	563	—	—	—
Trichocaulon	306	—	877	1195	—
Trichocereus	56	—	—	939	—
Uebelmannia	—	—	—	—	1308
Utahia	—	—	674	—	—
Weingartia	110	—	—	1008	—
Werckleocereus	—	—	—	—	1259
Wigginsia (was *Malacocarpus*)	—	—	—	—	—
Wilcoxia	63	—	619	—	—
Xerosycios	—	—	884	—	—
Zygocactus (*Schlumbergera*)	155	—	712	1035	—